THREE SLOVAK WOMEN

by
Lisa A. Alzo

D1509522

Gateway Press
Baltimore, MD
2003

First paperback edition 2001
Second printing, Baltimore, 2001
Third printing, Baltimore, 2002
Fourth printing, Baltimore, 2002
Fifth printing, Baltimore, 2003

For more information about this work, please visit the
Three Slovak Women Web site:
www.members.tripod.com/tswbook

Library of Congress Catalog Card Number 2001 129084

ISBN: 0-9710637-0-2

E-book version
ISBN: 0-9700492-8-5

Cover design by Lisa A. Alzo

Published for the author by
Gateway Press, Inc.
1001 N. Calvert St.
Baltimore, MD 21202

Manufactured in the United States of America

Dedicated to my mother and father

PREFACE

Nearly two million Americans claim Slovak ancestry. I am one of them. This vast number is not surprising given that some 600,000[1] Slovaks came to North America between 1875 and 1914. The Slovaks have been counted among the category of new immigrants called "Slavs," originating from central and east Europe and speaking a Slavic language. The terms "Slav" and "Slavic" are generic terms used to refer to a people of a number of different nationalities including Poles, Croats, Czech, Slovenians, and Ukranians who are bound together by a family of languages and cultures, which actually contain marked differences and have tended to be blurred in the United States. The Slavs were the third largest group to immigrate to the United States during that period, ranking only behind the Italian and Jewish immigrants. Out of the Slav-speaking groups in the United States, the Slovaks are the second largest, outnumbered only by the Poles.

Some Slovaks emigrated for economic reasons, others to escape political repression. The majority of the immigrants to the United States arrived before World War I. Many returned home after earning enough money to buy land back home, but eventually some 500,000 Slovaks settled permanently in the New World. If given voice, their stories could be both compelling and engaging, yet few have been told.

Despite the influx of Slovak immigrants to this country in the late 19th and early 20th centuries, there is a definite lack of Slovak identity in early American literature. This could possibly be explained by the generalized view of American society at the turn of the century that Slovaks were poor, downtrodden or full of misery. Such stereotypes emerged and remained due primarily to prejudice from the Irish hierarchy of the Catholic church. In addition, the unions excluded the less skilled and undereducated,

---

[1] Figure closer to 620,000. Fourteenth Census of the United States. Taken in the year 1920, Vol. II, Population: General Report and Analytical Tables, (Washington, 1922): 984.

non-English speaking peasants, indignantly labeled as "Hunkies." The etymology of the term "Hunky" comes from the original reference to Slovaks as "Huns," (in reference to Attila the Hun and his Asiatic followers) by those who were disgusted by these immigrants' cramped living quarters, and would even precede the term with the words, "miserable" or "murderous." The slur had its origins with those early Slovak immigrants who settled in the Northeastern and Midwestern states, particularly in and around industrial centers such as Pittsburgh, Cleveland and Chicago. Slovak immigrants lived in the poorest neighborhoods, typically in those places abandoned by the Irish. The Irish taunted the Slavs because they believed these new immigrants would take away their jobs. Eventually "Hun" was softened to "Hunky," and was the name given to a foreigner or immigrant laborer, first made popular in Pennsylvania when singling out Hungarian, Lithuanian, and Slavic workers. "Hunky" was often interchanged with "Bohunk," formed from two other words: Bohemian and Hungarian, and reinforced by the derogatory word, "hunk" and meant a stupid or clumsy person.

There was an even more serious form of prejudice toward Slavic immigrants than the ethnic slurs hurled at them by the Irish or other groups. A group of young Harvard graduates, and wealthy Bostonians, alarmed by the influx of new arrivals from Eastern Europe, formed the Immigrant Restriction League (1890 - 1924), to help develop laws to exclude those considered "undesirables." Such groups had friends in high places, who shared their views. Even Senator Henry Cabot Lodge has been quoted as saying, "The Slavic immigrant threatened to contaminate America."

Such real-life stereotypes were further reflected in literature. In the book, *American Xenophobia and the Slavic Immigrant*, Josephine Wtulich explains that in about 100 works published between 1900 and 1965 (written by members of the host society and not by immigrants or hyphenated Americans), the Slav portrayed is often the Pole. She writes, "With very few exceptions, these works appeared on the American literary scene during the period that roughly coincides with the heavy immigration of Slavs from central and east Europe. In them are depicted the life experiences of Slavs in the twentieth century who had been defined as the new immigrants." Furthermore, it seems that novels and short stories written for both adults and juveniles during this period, provide stereotypical images of the Slav. In juvenile literature (such as Tom Swift or Nancy Drew), the protagonist was always a White Anglo-Saxon Protestant (WASP) and the antagonist a foreigner, and immigrant, and sometimes specified as a Slav. In adult fiction, the image of the Slav, whether man, woman, worker or priest is generally overloaded with negative stereotypes, and often the Slav is used as a symbol or as the representative ethnic. For example, in Upton Sinclair's novel, *The Jungle* (1905), Slovak voices are indistinguishable, being blended into a chorus of other Eastern European groups. The Slovaks were shown as the newest immigrant group, forced to endure a dismal existence just as the other immigrants who had preceded them. As Sinclair wrote: "The Bohemians had come, and after them the Poles. The Poles [who had come by tens of thousands] had been driven to the wall by the Lithuanians, and now the Lithuanians were giving way to the Slovaks. Who there was poorer and more miserable than the Slovaks, Grandmother Majauszkis had no idea..."

In a 1985 essay, dealing with the Slovak immigrant's view of work, Patricia Ondek Laurence asserted that "Prejudice, stereotypes, and 'silence' about Slovaks persist even today because no writer of Slovak-American heritage has achieved significant stature in American literature to carry the voice and images of Slovaks into the mainstream." In fact, according to this writer, only a small body of Slovak immigrant literature (about 15 works) focusing on the turn-of-the-century immigrant experience is available in English. Among such written works are Father Andrew Pier's autobiography, *The Woodlands Above, the Mines Below* (1975), which describes his family's life among the mines in the small town of Blandburg, Pennsylvania; Thames Williamson's *Hunky* (1929) about a Slovak worker in a bakery; and finally, Thomas Bell's *Out of This Furnace* (1941), the classic novel which chronicles the lives of three generations of Slovak men working in the steel mills of Braddock, Pennsylvania.

In reviewing each of these poignant works, I noticed that a strong emphasis is placed on the Slovak immigrant male, whose daily existence was a mere backdrop to the work he did in those places most familiar to him—the mills and the mines. For it was there, in the depths of the black pits or near the chasm of the hot blast furnaces, that the Slovak male performed the backbreaking tasks of digging the coal that provided fuel or producing the metal and steel which were the signature materials of industrial growth.

In early literature, only Bell's book mentions, in any detail, the Slovak woman. In one section of his book entitled "Mary," he devotes 50 pages to the thoughts, struggles and daily activities of Mary Dobrechak, who was first generation American. The focus on the woman, however, is still secondary to the overall story of the three men. We see Mary as a widow who is left to deal with life after her husband is killed in the mill. She is shown taking up where her husband left off in trying to support herself and her children and is enthusiastically encouraged to marry again rather than make it on her own. With Mary, Bell gives us a glimpse— albeit a moving and accurate one—into the lives of Slovak women who served not only as the money handlers by controlling the family's finances, but who also became the backbone of the family with responsibility for rearing their children. These women performed work that was not only tedious and endless, but also essential.

After reading Bell's book several years ago, I yearned to know more about all of the other "Mary's" that life and literature had left by the wayside.

Except for general history books dealing with immigrants, and the occasional collection of biographies in which she is counted among women from various other ethnic groups, I have come across only a few modern and contemporary works concentrating on the Slovak immigrant woman: *Icon of Spring* by Sonjya Jason (1993), an autobiographic account of a young Slovak girl's coming of age as a first generation American and her discovery that she is really a "Rusyn" and not a Slovak; the fictional *Sorrows of Marienka*, by Vasil Koban (1979), which follows a young girl from her wedding in Slovakia through her subsequent immigration to America, and *Grandmothers, Mothers and Daughters: Oral Histories of Three Generations of Ethnic American Women*, by Corinne Krause (1991) documents the experiences of Jewish, Italian and Slavic women who came to America's shores, as well as the stories of these women's daughters and granddaughters.

I can only speculate as to the reasons why a comparatively small number of texts have been written about the Slovak immigrant woman. Perhaps these females thought their lives unimportant or unworthy of mentioning, or perhaps the mere struggle for day-to-day survival left them with little time to concern themselves with writing their memoirs. In a foreword written for the book, *The Immigrant Experience in American Fiction*, Teresa Kanoza asserts that most fiction set between 1890-1914, which happened to be the largest stage of the Mediterranean-Slavic wave of the great migration, was written not by immigrants themselves, but by their children and grandchildren. She notes that it usually took a generation or two before an ethnic-American family produced a writer. She attributes this pattern of authorship to the circumstances surrounding removal and relocation and to the type of immigrants who arrived at the turn of the century, or as she refers to them as the "new" or non-Protestant/non-Christian immigrants as opposed to the "old" immigrants who came predominantly from northern and western Europe between 1815 and 1890. The "new" immigrants were peasants, artisans and shopkeepers who came to escape the economic, political or religious oppression of their homelands. "As a result, many who immigrated at the turn of the last century were consumed by the tasks of providing for their families and trying to save money to bring over more family members or to return home to buy land. They often lacked the time or know-how to create written literature; some were literate neither in English nor their native language." Thus, if these were obstacles to writing for immigrants in general, then it stands to reason that they were even more profound for those women who stayed at home and had little exposure to the English language or formal education.

A third possibility is that Slovak women were not viewed by others as significant contributors to this country's history. As women, they were already looked upon as minorities, but they had a double strike against them because they were also foreigners.

Some documented sources put forth an interesting theory: before 1965 most traditional historians considered the immigrant to be a "problem" that could only be solved by assimilation, leaving the ethnic American to fall victim to discrimination. Much of the literature on immigration has, in general, centered on the male, taking men's experiences as the norm and assuming that women's experiences were either identical to the men's or not important enough to warrant separate and serious attention. The distinctive experiences of immigrant women were usually placed under men's history or treated with indifference or condescension. Women were forced into the background by cultural and societal barriers. In the case of Slovak women in particular, the family was patriarchal in nature, with its age-old practice of male domination and the belief that the man was the boss. Since women were typically undervalued in traditional Slavic culture, it is plausible to assume that contemporary literature reflected such treatment in society. While I have not found any definitive statements to corroborate this assumption for "Slovak" women, Paul R. Magocsi in his book, *Rusyn-American Ethnic Literature*, does talk of the portrayal of women in Rusyn-American literature. The Rusyns once inhabited portions of several counties in Northeast Hungary and like the Slavs, came to America as part of the massive, pre-World War I immigration from eastern and southern Europe. Regarding the treatment of women in Rusyn culture, Magocsi writes: "Women are disparagingly treated. In almost all instances describing male-female relationships, the courtship stage is marked with promises by the suitor that he will give his fiancée everything in life. After marriage, however, the standard characterization reveals a disrespectful husband who treats his passive wife as chattel and can only address her as the old lady (*stara*) or grandma (*baba*)."

It was not until the late 1960s and early 1970s, however, that two movements emerged to alter the way in which female immigrants were viewed: the rise of a "new ethnicity" and the revival of the women's movement. As a result, many scholars began to rethink the way they approached the history of immigration in general and the history of women in particular. Whatever the reasons for the lack of written accounts documenting the lives of Slovak immigrant women in the past, I believe it is both illuminating and important for some stories to finally be told. This does not mean that the men should be completely forgotten, because they indeed played pivotal roles in shaping such women's lives. Rather, these early Slovak women immigrants need to be shown as human beings who had their own feelings, hopes, dreams and desires. Their stories are personal and at the same time universal—a genuinely human representation of 20th century American history. For this reason, if none other, Slovak immigrant women must somehow find their place in historical literature.

It was with this concept in mind that I decided to write a story about three Slovak women. My grandmother came to America from Slovakia in the early 20th century. She left behind the world most familiar to her to make a new home in America. Yet in all the time that I spent with her before she died, I never thought about her as someone who had her own identity or interesting stories to tell. I saw her only as my grandmother. Until a few years ago, I knew nothing about her life as a young girl back in Slovakia, the story of how and why she came to America, or her experiences as an immigrant trying to survive in a culture that was new and different from her own. In this respect, my grandmother was no different from the other Slovak women whose stories were never told. I want to be the one to finally tell her story, perhaps not in the way she would have told it had she been given the opportunity, and maybe not as eloquently as she deserves. But I hope that my account will capture her experiences as accurately as possible to show, above all else, that she mattered.

In order to tell my grandmother's full story, I must also explore how her experiences and choices as a young woman— what she thought and did—ultimately influenced not only her daughter's (my mother's) life but also that of her granddaughter (me). My grandmother's influence was undoubtedly a profound one that created lasting ties and affectionate bonds between the generations, as I would hope the influence of other immigrant women did for their own families.

Keeping in mind the idea of the mother-daughter bonds and conflicts, I am led to speculate that perhaps this is why the burden of telling this story rests with me. I often have wondered why my mother never felt inspired to document her mother's life or even her own. In various oral histories, the intimacy as well as the conflict, especially between immigrant mothers and their daughters are revealed in the interviews. Such conflicts most often arose from the attempts of successive generations to break through cultural barriers and discover their own identities as Slovak-Americans. Many daughters of immigrants—those born in this country—expressed a strong desire to be real Americans and lose their ethnic identities. In spite of the conflicts, the second generation still maintained an attachment to their Slovak culture and the ties between the women remained strong. The language barriers or cultural differences that separated the generations in the early period of immigration were not as pronounced, and strong bonds formed between the first and third generations, despite the wide gaps in experience.

These gaps can be explained with reference to assimilation. Moreover, as many third generation Slovaks, like myself, move away from the ethnic neighborhoods where the first generation settled, many of us find ourselves separating from the Slovak culture and its richly embedded traditions. I find myself fully acclimated to a way of life that goes far beyond the pursuit of the "American dream" which encompassed my mother's and grandmother's generations. For them, that dream centered around the desire to own a house or a piece of land, or to earn enough money to ensure that their children had a better start at life than they had themselves. Today, I easily take for granted numerous things my grandmother and mother did not have, such as my college education, owning a car, the simple enjoyment of listening to my favorite modern music on a compact disc player. I am comfortable with my American lifestyle and white-collar job. But every now and then I get the urge to pause, to take a break from my technologically advanced world of cellular telephones and computers. Once disconnected from those tools, which serve as my lifeline to the outside world, I often find myself thinking about what my grandmother experienced. In stepping back, I am also compelled to consider what values I may have compromised in order to adapt, or what traditions have been forgotten along the way. In trying to get a clear picture of who I am, I need to see my grandmother for who she was. I want to understand and appreciate her so that I will be able to document the events of her life, which must not be viewed as isolated incidents, but as the catalysts that shaped the lives of future generations. After all, those things she taught her children and grandchildren are priceless: family solidarity, religious faith, and continuity of the ethnic tradition. Because of all these things my grandmother taught me, I want to ensure that she does not remain a part of a neglected chapter of American history.

One of the difficulties in telling this story is that like many descendants of early immigrants, the interest came too little, too late. I missed the opportunity to ask my grandmother anything about her life or to record her stories first-hand. Perhaps if I had listened more attentively or had asked more questions, maybe even had a tape recorder on hand, I would not be at such a loss as to how to document the life of this woman who was more than just my grandmother. Unfortunately I let the opportunity slip by while she was still alive and her own personal account has been lost forever. For the most part, my grandmother did not volunteer much information and the little she did tell her children, I have attempted to record here. I want to give voice to her silence.

As time passes I see my heritage slowly slipping from memory. My grandmother's language is rarely spoken and the holiday traditions she piously followed are being abandoned as I have adopted more modern American ways of celebration, ways that are not concerned with religious rituals and cultural traditions, but focus more on the material world (of presents and holiday parties). Thus, in my own way, I want to preserve that heritage, and have something to pass on to future generations, not only for the benefit of my own family, but also for other descendants of immigrants who may know nothing of their own ancestors' lives.

In telling my grandmother's story, I had to discover the facts through careful research, use of documents, and the recollection of others, particularly my mother, who served as the bridge, the one who communicated to me as best she could, the answers to my questions about my grandmother's life. She shared her own story about being a first generation American and growing up in a home where the ways of the old country and the discoveries of the new often clashed. My mother became the middle link in a chain of three generations of Slovak women. We all share the same heritage, come from the same blood, but each is different. Connected, yet separate.

But there is a difficulty in trying to recreate the past. There are so many details that have been lost. The weaving together of details known and unknown is like trying to build a puzzle, with some of the pieces missing. This too, is part of the story.

AUTHOR'S NOTE

While the author is cognizant that her heritage may be identified as Carpatho-Rusyn and/or possibly Ukrainian, her grandparents chose to identify themselves as "Slovak." All family documents and resources list Verona Straka and Jánoš Figlyar as "Slovak" with regard to ethnic identity. The book is written as a family testimonial and is not intended as a tool for political causes related to any particular group whether Czech, Rusyn, Slovak, Ukrainian or any others.

In addition, as is typically the case with genealogical research, there is always the possibility of discovering new and/or contradictory facts about one's ancestors. This edition includes changes and updates in family information I have uncovered in the never-ending search for my roots.

ACKNOWLEDGMENTS

I am deeply grateful to the following individuals who helped to make the completion of this book possible:

My grandmother, Veronica Straka Figlar (1899-1984) who was the inspiration for this story; my other three grandparents (John Figlar 1896-1974, John Alzo 1894-1961) and Elizabeth Fencak Alzo 1898-1966) for the personal courage and determination to leave their homeland and start a new life in America; my parents, John and Anna Figlar Alzo (deceased, September 12, 2000) for their love, support and encouragement, my aunts and uncles: John Figlar (deceased), Joseph Figlar, Michael Figlar, Helen Figlar Lizanov, Geraldine Figlar Abbott, Margaret Figlar Augenstein and their spouses, and my cousins (too many to list individually); my husband, Michael; my instructors in the Creative Nonfiction program, Department of English, University of Pittsburgh: Patsy Sims, James Conaway, Nicholas Coles, and Bruce Dobler for their patience and guidance during my years in the program.

I would like to extend a special thank you to Ann Hughes and Gateway Press, Baltimore, MD, for her assistance in putting this story into print.

I would also like to specifically thank the following individuals for their assistance in providing information for this project (listed alphabetically): Elizabeth Berta (deceased), Rich Custer, Mary Figler (deceased), Emily Ivak, Members of the Kolcun and Gereg families, Megan Smolenyak, Mike Smolenak, Members of St. Nicholas Church, Barton, Ohio, Mrs. Mary Yuhasz (deceased), and anyone else I may have inadvertently overlooked.

Finally, I am grateful to Dr. Michael J. Kopanic, Jr., and Professor Steven Várdy for their expertise and guidance with the text changes and historical references for this current edition.

CHAPTER ONE
VERONA

She was often called Veronica, although her given name was Verona. I called her "Grandma." She came to America in 1922 via Ellis Island, just as some 6,000 other Slovak immigrants did that year. It was four years after the end of World War I, one year after the U.S. Congress passed the first Immigration Quota Law restricting the number of any European nationality that could enter the country on an annual basis. Grandma was among those fortunate enough to clear this restriction. Each immigrant had his or her own reason for coming to America: some to escape poverty and political or religious oppression, others to seek employment. While these men and women had in common the universal experiences surrounding emigration from their home land, each individual also had his or her own story to tell. My grandmother was no different.

She was born on November 10, 1899, the youngest of twelve children born to Maria Verbosky and Andrej [ON-DRAY] Straka, a peasant farmer who lived in the village of Milpos, in the western part of Saris County, Slovakia. Like many other small villages throughout Slovakia, Milpos consisted mainly of farmland, some 15-20 homes and a small church. Its inhabitants, including my grandmother's family, came from peasant backgrounds, and historically from a feudal society. Feudal lords owned the land and kept the majority of crops for their own use. These lords provided land to the peasants or serfs to cultivate and live on, but their crops were turned over to the lord at harvest time. It was not until 1848, during the time of the Hungarian revolution (and some 50 years before my grandmother's birth), that feudalism was finally abolished.

With the end of feudalism, those peasants who found themselves landless were left with few prospects for employment. The Hungarian rulers, who did little to remedy the situation failed to embrace industrialization, which may have helped to ease this problem. The lack of employment combined with epidemics of

1

cholera, trachoma, tuberculosis and typhus during the 1850s and a series of crop failures and droughts in the 1860s contributed to the already poor living conditions.

So, with a lack of resources, Slovaks began to look outside the country for employment opportunities; not long afterwards, the great migrations began. America was especially appealing. Due to the boom of industrialization, America needed strong men to work in its factories, mines and mills. Steamship agents enticed many laborers from Slovakia by telling marvelous stories, through handbills and newspapers, of how America was a land of plenty, where higher wages, economic and social advantage awaited those who came to its shores.

From the 10th century right up to 1918 Slovakia had been part of the Kingdom of Hungary. In the 16th century Hungary (including Slovakia) became an associated state of the Habsburg Empire (ruled by the Habsburg family). Between 1804 and 1867 the Habsburg Empire was renamed Austrian Empire. Between 1867 and 1918 the Austrian Empire was restructured into a dualist state called Austria-Hungary, with each state having its own army, government, parliament, and citizenship.[2]

At the time of Grandma's birth, Slovakia was one of two provinces controlled by the dual monarchy of Austria-Hungary and its repressive Hapsburg ruler, the Emperor Francis [Franz] Joseph I (Emperor of Austria from 1848-1916 and King of Hungary from 1867-1916). The Czech territories belonged to the Austrian part of the Hapsburg monarchy, while the Slovak territories belonged to the Hungarian part. Economically, the Czech lands were the most developed. The Slovak territories were cut off from economic development by the political border between Austria and Hungary, and from the north by the Carpathian mountain range. This made it tough for the Slovak people, because they were bound politically to the Hungarian government. While the Czech and Slovak

---

[2] Professor Steven Várdy, e-mail communication, March 2003.

cultures are somewhat similar, eastern Slovak culture is much different than Czech and more similar to the Polish or Ukrainian.[3]

During the early part of the 19th century, the Slovak economy grew slowly due to worldwide economic slumps and also because the Industrial Revolution came later to Slovakia than to Western Europe and the Czech lands. Thus while the Czech lands were more advanced and industrialized, Slovakia remained a backward area, primarily based on agriculture. As a result, Slovak immigration to the United States increased rapidly at the end of the nineteenth century as many Slovaks became more and more dissatisfied with local conditions. By 1900, Slovakia had lost over 300,000 of its inhabitants to emigration.

My great-grandfather was not lured by the promise of luxuries and comfort, which supposedly waited across the ocean. While I am unsure of the exact reason he chose to stay in Slovakia when so many other men opted for America, I can only speculate that Andrej Straka must have been among the few who could afford to buy a small plot of land. Although a poor farmer, he somehow managed to earn a modest living as a tailor which, at that time, was considered the occupation of choice. Andrej's specialty was sewing military uniforms which he delivered on foot to nearby villages like Krivany, Hanigovce and Lipany.

The family lived in a timber chalet typical of peasant villages. The house was built from uncut logs, had a thatched roof and perhaps two or three windows in a row facing the village street. The interior consisted of only one room, approximately 15' square, with a dirt floor and a stove built into one corner. There were no beds. Instead bunks were built around the room for some of the family, while the rest slept in a small loft. In the winter the only heat came from a stove. A shallow cellar underneath the house provided a place to store vegetables, milk and other basic supplies. Without the convenience of an indoor bathroom, the family used the ground outside.

---

[3] The word "Czecho-Slovak" was first used during the First World War and eventually turned into a movement lead by Masaryk to create a new nationality known as the "Czechoslovaks." Dr. Michael J. Kopanic, Jr., personal communication 2003.

As peasants the family lived off the land. Their food consisted of whatever they could get from the livestock they raised: milk from the cows and eggs from the chickens. Fresh fruit and vegetables were practically non-existent except for cabbage and potatoes, which could successfully be grown in their small garden and were the staples that made up their diet. To buy hay or feed for the animals, they sold butter or other items. Once a year, usually in the fall, they would slaughter a pig, which when cured, often provided enough meat and bacon to last them for the year.

Since he was a tailor, Andrej was able to make the family's clothing. I can picture him, needle and thread in hand, as he sewed shirts, blouses, ornate bodices, skirts, aprons, trousers and vests by hand from bleached linen cloth, decorating the cuffs and collars with embroidery, lace, and brightly colored ribbons. Most of the time both men and women walked around barefoot because shoes had to be made and the family could not afford such a luxury, unless it was for a special occasion such as a wedding.

My grandmother's girlhood, like that of most young Slavic girls, was short-lived.

In general, everyone in the family shared in the responsibilities of running a household and farm. Young girls were trained to work in the fields at an early age because there were not enough men to do the work. Male family members were either called away to the military or left their homeland for America. In my grandmother's case, three of her four brothers, Michael, Matias (Martin) and Andrew had left for the United States and one brother, Istvan, served in the Hungarian army.

Verona learned how to work from watching her mother. Typically, she would rise early each morning to go out and work in the fields. She would gather the wheat, which had to be ground, by hand, through a mill, to make the flour used to bake bread. In addition to working in the fields, Verona learned basic housekeeping duties from her mother: cooking, cleaning, sewing, weaving and dressmaking. She had to be skilled in all aspects of caring for a home so that she would be prepared for marriage. With such long and tedious work, it is no wonder that back in those

4

days, the Slovak mother was considered an old woman by the time her eldest daughter got married.

There is a photograph of my great-grandma—one my grandmother brought with her to America that was eventually passed down to me. I estimate that great-grandma must have been in her late 50s or early 60s at the time the photo was taken, but she looks much older. Her face is sunken with wrinkles surrounding her dark, lifeless eyes and she is not smiling. I can see years of toil on her face. She has the look of a woman who has endured life, but not enjoyed it. There is a sadness, which can be read in her eyes. My great-grandmother at 50 looked almost as old as I remember my grandmother looked when she was 70.

The capacity for hard work was not the only thing my grandmother learned from her mother. From her, Verona also learned to have a deep faith in God. For Slovaks, religion was above all in importance since the time Christianity was brought to the area (then known as Great Moravia) in 863 A.D., by two Byzantine monks, Cyril and Methodius, who eventually became known as the "Apostles to the Slavs." Over the course of the next several centuries, grand churches of various faiths, Roman or Greek Catholic, Orthodox and Evangelical Lutheran, began to develop in villages throughout Slovakia. Religious symbols were visible as soon as one came upon a village: a wooden cross typically marked the village's entrance, and many shrines were built throughout to honor Jesus and Mary. Slovak woman made frequent church visits, and the church was the place where all of life's significant events such as baptisms, weddings and funerals took place.

My grandmother was baptized and raised in the Greek Catholic (or Uniate) church founded somewhere between 1596 and 1646. In 1054 an official split took place between Rome and Constantinople, (the Catholic Church and the Eastern Orthodox Church). Most of the Balkan Slavs (Bulgarians, Serbians, etc.) and the Eastern Slavs (Russians, Ukrainians, Belorussians, Rusyns,) were Christianized by Constantinople in the 9th and 10th centuries. Many of these Orthodox Christians, under various political pressures, later united or reunited with Rome. Many of the

Ukrainians and Belorussians united with Rome at the Union of Brest of 1596. The Rusyns united with Rome at the Union of Ungvár/Uzhgorod/Uzhhorod of 1646. It was because of these unions that they became Greek Catholics (Uniates) or Byzantine Catholics, as they are known in the United States since the late 1920s.[4]

Each rite followed its own traditions. The Eastern Christians followed the liturgy of St. John Chrysotom and used Church Slavonic rather than the Latin language in their services, received both bread and wine at Communion, followed the Julian calendar instead of the Gregorian calendar (which meant that feasts such as Christmas fell two weeks later), and permitted their priests to marry. At the time my grandmother was growing up, the Greek Catholics were one of the smaller religious groups in Slovakia.

After religion, family life was next in importance to the Slovak people. Families were often extended. Parents, grandparents, children, aunts, uncles, cousins and in-laws lived under one roof. While growing up, Verona was the closest to her brothers, Istvan and Andrew, and her niece, Mary, the illegitimate daughter of Verona's eldest sister, Maria.

Maria had gone to America when Mary was an infant, leaving the baby in the care of her grandparents. The baby's father was rumored to be a Catholic priest from the local village whom Maria had worked for as a housekeeper. Back in the old country, in spite of strong religious mores, it occasionally happened that a single girl became pregnant. Pregnancy before marriage was considered a shame not only for the immediate family but also for the whole village. In most instances, a wedding ceremony was arranged as soon as possible before the woman's pregnancy became visible.

In Maria's case, no such arrangement was made. Although in the Greek Catholic faith priests were permitted to marry, family stories never revealed why in Maria's case a marriage failed to take place. To avoid the shame of having a child out of wedlock, Maria

---

[4] Professor Steven Várdy, e-mail communication, March 2003.

departed for America immediately after the baby was born. The family claimed the priest paid for the ticket.

Since Mary was only six years younger than Verona, the two shared a relationship more characteristic of sisters than aunt and niece. They performed chores together; they tended to the family's cabbage and potato patch, grazed the sheep, milked the cows and fed the chickens and geese. With all the work to be done around the house, there was little time for schooling. The girls received only the mandatory elementary education, enough to learn how to read and write (my grandmother attended up until fifth grade), and as was the requirement under Franz Joseph, were taught the Hungarian language.

This teaching of the Hungarian language was but one attempt by Hungarian officials to "Magyarize," or force the Magyar culture onto the Slovak peoples, in hopes of spreading the Hungarian influence and preserving the empire. This explains why all of my Grandmother's important documents were in Hungarian.

Despite the Hungarian influence, many Slovak families, such as my grandmother's, tried hard to maintain their traditions and language privately at home since they were forbidden to do so publicly. Some Slovaks were so desperate to save their families or intent on keeping their heritage intact that they sought refuge in America, with some 33,000 Slovaks leaving their homeland between 1910 and 1914. Despite the attempts of the Hungarians to eradicate the Slovak culture, my great-grandparents were among those who preferred their homeland to emigration.

It is difficult to imagine my grandmother as a young woman. In a black and white photograph of her and Mary, the only photograph I have of her at this age, Grandma is small in stature. She is wearing a skirt and vest over a blouse with puffy sleeves. Two thin strips of patterned material are tied in front of the skirt, accentuating her thick waist, wide hips and well-developed breasts. Her dark hair is pulled away from her face into a braid and fastened at the back of her head with a comb. Her eyes (described in her passport as "blue") are slanted at the corners, and she has a small, round nose and thin pursed lips. In her face I see a look of determination. Mary, dressed identically, appears several

7

inches shorter than Grandma and slightly more petite. Her arm is resting on Grandma's shoulder. In the photo, her hair appears a shade darker, but is pulled back, in the same fashion as Grandma's, away from her thin, oblong face.

The girls were quite young when the Archduke Francis Ferdinand, heir to the Austro-Hungarian thrones was assassinated by a Serbian nationalist during a visit to Sarajevo in June 1914, setting off the First World War. Verona was barely a teenager, and Mary was only eight years old. The war lasted four years, during which immigration to America declined significantly because passage out of Slovakia was difficult, if not impossible.

The war exacerbated the barely tolerable conditions under which my grandmother's family lived. To make matters worse, a worldwide flu epidemic struck between 1917 and 1919, eventually killed an estimated 20-30 million people. Verona caught the flu after walking outdoors in a bitter winter storm. She lapsed into a coma for several days and almost died. Later, when she told her children about the illness, she said the wind felt like it blew straight through her ears and swore that was the reason she had trouble with her ears most of her life. With only one doctor in the village, and no modern medications, the family relied on home remedies to cure such illnesses. For colds they would grease the sick person with goose fat and put them to bed. For sore throats they would fry garlic in goose lard, then add milk to make a drink, or mix up another concoction of whiskey, honey and garlic. Pneumonia and diphtheria were treated by drinking kerosene with sugar in it, or straight whiskey. The home remedies, however, failed to cure Verona's father. He had suffered frostbite and hypothermia, which resulted from walking in the snow as he made his uniform deliveries. Complications set in and eventually caused his death.

During the pandemic, World War I was coming to an end. In 1918 the Allies went on to victory, and on October 28 of that year, the Czechs and Slovaks formed their own republic. My grandmother was 19 when Czechoslovakia came into existence as a nation. The unification was a result of the revolutionary action of the people in the two provinces, and the end of the war, which

8

ended in the disintegration of the Austro-Hungarian Empire. The new Republic consisted of Bohemia, Moravia, and Silesia (the Czech-speaking Austrian provinces), a small section of Prussian Silesia, the Northern area of old Hungary, called Slovakia (Slovak-speaking areas) and the northeastern section of old Hungary also known as Ruthenia (inhabited by people who spoke Rusin, a Ukrainian dialect still spoken today).

In spite of the newfound unity, the country succumbed to a worldwide postwar depression, and the province of Slovakia was severely stricken. After the war, economic resources dwindled and food was scarce, with items such as flour, sugar, milk, meat in short supply. The war devastated agriculture as soil went uncultivated because the male workforce and horses were drafted by the army. Furthermore, a potato shortage (potatoes were the mainstay of the Slovak diet), and the departure of large estate owners harmed the Slovak agriculture. Hunger was prevalent and unemployment became a reality for those soldiers who returned home from war or from abroad to find no jobs available. The government was unable to assist because it had to keep the army ready for another possible attack from Hungary.

From 1921-1923, the Slovak economy suffered a severe depression; world trade declined, workers were laid off from factories and businesses closed. It was during this period that my grandmother made the decision to leave her homeland. Family stories reveal, however, that it was primarily because of her niece, Mary, that she made the journey at all.

Letters arrived periodically from Mary's mother who had married a man named Michael Shivak, a widower with three children who worked in a steel mill near Pittsburgh, Pennsylvania, one of the major industrial cities in America.

When Mary was sixteen she received a letter from her mother that would change her life as well as Verona's. It is not known whether or not Mary knew the actual circumstances behind her mother's departure all those years ago, but this letter indicated that Maria could now afford to support her daughter and invited her to America. Mary feared making the journey alone, so she asked Verona to accompany her and Maria paid for both tickets.

My grandmother was the last sibling to leave home. Four sisters besides Maria—Katherine, Sophie, Elizabeth and Susan—and her brothers Michael, Mathias (Martin) and Andrew had already settled in the United States, in towns throughout Ohio and Pennsylvania. After watching seven of her children leave home already, Verona's mother now had to watch her youngest leave for America, possibly never to see her again. It must have been equally difficult for Verona to leave her mother and brothers behind, but there was not much for her to look forward to if she stayed. The war and previous mass emigration had depleted many of the small villages, like Milpos, of young, single men. In fact, between 1869 and 1890, Saris County lost 34 percent of the men between the ages of 20-25 and 44 percent of men between 26-30. Consequently, this left women of Verona's age with very slim chances of finding a husband.

The conditions of a peasant life were also tied to century-old social barriers, and despite the fact that during the war many women either took the places of men or worked side by side with them in the fields, they were never regarded as equals. Furthermore, the prospects for employment were not good for young landless women. In fact, they had but two occupational choices: they could either work on farms that paid a meager 25¢ per day, or they could go into domestic service, where they would be forced to work 12-hour days, often non-stop, and even on Sunday. Domestic work meant doing housework both inside and outside, and included such chores as spreading fertilizer on the fields throughout the hot summers or during the cold and snowy winters. Stories that came from America told of how domestic service there paid more. Work in America held the promise of a greater reward.

Most young women were motivated to improve their economic status, and many went as part of a family or, in the case of Verona and Mary, to join relatives already in America. Verona's mother encouraged Verona to leave.

Once the decision to leave was made, much time and effort went into planning for the journey. The girls had to get shots and apply for passports and other official papers. Typically several months elapsed between the time the decision was made and the date of departure. My grandmother waited approximately four months. Emigrants typically obtained their passports in the city closest to where the family resided. For Grandma, it was Présov. Her passport was issued on March 16, 1922. The following July, she and Mary set off in a peasant wagon from Milpos. Whether or not they had any knowledge of the dangers they might encounter along the way or considered the possibility they might be turned back once they arrived and would not admitted to America at all, I do not know, but most likely they did realize that they might never see their homeland again.

As was custom, the whole town came to say good-bye. Family and friends gathered in the center of town, said prayers for a safe journey for the two young women, and exchanged hugs and kisses with them. The residents of the village then walked behind the wagon, and followed the girls to the village border and bid them a tearful farewell.

CHAPTER TWO
ARRIVING IN AMERICA

As the last glimpse of Milpos disappeared behind them, Verona and Mary faced the realization that they were now truly on their own. They journeyed by train from village to village until they reached Présov, where they boarded another train for Hamburg, Germany.

During the early immigration years, Slovak men initially went to America alone. Those first immigrants typically did not take their wives and children with them, since most went to earn money and then planned to return to Slovakia to buy land. The wife would remain in the old country to tend to the land and raise the children. Later on fewer men returned, but instead would establish quarters in America and then send for the women and children. By the last two decades of the nineteenth century, however, women had the task of shepherding their families to the new world. After 1900, with the number of single young men depleted, the number of marriages declined in Slovakia. After the First World War, Slovak women eventually began to follow the pattern set by the Irish of sending single women over to America to establish a home. Thus at the time Verona and Mary headed for America, it was not unusual for two single young women to make the journey on their own.

Once in Hamburg, Verona and Mary were in the hands of the steamship company. The companies were required to conduct health inspections of all prospective passengers, and Verona and Mary went through the routine: they were deloused through antiseptic baths and their clothing and baggage fumigated. While awaiting departure, they stayed in a seaport hotel in dormitory-style rooms paid for by the steamship company. The average stay in the port was approximately four days. Thirty-six hours before departure, they were deloused again and moved to the "clean" side of the hotel. Next, officials interrogated them about who they were and their destination before they were permitted to purchase their tickets. Then finally on July 26, 1922, they boarded the 15,507 ton steamship *Orduna* and set sail for America.

The size of the large ocean liner must have impressed the two women upon first sight. Once aboard, however, any notions of magnificence surely would have faded. Like the majority of immigrants who sailed on these North Atlantic liners, Verona and Mary traveled steerage class, the least expensive and most uncomfortable way to travel, but the most profitable for the company as steerage ships could carry nearly 1,000 people at a time.

Verona and Mary spent most of the trip near the bottom of the ship in semi-darkness, with no portholes and little ventilation. They either slept on straw or a thin mattress laid upon two- or three-tiered bunk racks. The toilet facilities were just plain openings above the on-rushing sea, and bathing was nearly impossible; the showers were open stalls with rusted faucets through which only cold ocean water trickled. Passengers also had to endure the lack of privacy forced upon them by such close quarters.

Their food consisted of little more than thin soup, lean slices of beef, boiled potatoes, soggy rye bread and herring, which they ate from tin plates provided them upon boarding. Lice and vomit from seasick passengers added to the barely tolerable conditions. Mary was among those who became seasick during the journey, but Verona managed to escape the nausea and dizziness that afflicted many of her fellow passengers.

Such voyages were long, uncomfortable and at times fatal due to epidemics spread on board the vessels. Travel time on the steamships took, on average between 15 to 60 days, depending on weather conditions, and whether it was a direct or indirect route. Grandma's transatlantic journey lasted approximately 12 days with the ship sailing through the English and French ports of Southampton and Cherbourg until finally, on August 7th, the *Orduna* arrived in New York.

For many young people, such as my grandmother, the trip to America was the first time they traveled out beyond their own village. Throughout the journey, and especially once they reached

America, travelers often ate foods (such as bananas or oranges) they had never eaten.

The first glimpse of the United States was a joyous occasion. As many passengers as possible crowded onto the deck to see the Statue of Liberty. Little did the immigrants know what awaited them at the hands of immigration officials or health inspectors.

Once in the harbor, the *Orduna* anchored in the narrows and hoisted a yellow "quarantine" flag, as passenger ships routinely did. Immigration officials and doctors from the U.S. Public Health Service then boarded the ship to inspect the passengers for signs of disease—especially cholera, typhoid or yellow fever. After clearance, the ship continued through the narrows to the dock. Those immigrants who traveled first or second class were able to pass quickly through immigration inspection on board, and were permitted to exit the ship and then descend the gangways directly into the street. But, as steerage class passengers, Verona and Mary had to wait on the boat until they were called to the pier to board a small wooden ferry that would shuttle them in the sweltering August heat the final mile to Ellis Island. The wait may have been as long as several days.

As the two women disembarked from the ferry, they knew nothing of quota laws or the history of the red brick structure with limestone trim they were about to enter. Ellis Island, once a mere three and a half-acre mud bank, was named for Samuel Ellis who owned the island in the 1700s. Once called "Oyster Island" after its many surrounding oyster beds, Ellis Island eventually came under government control and functioned as an arsenal from the period prior to the War of 1812 up until 1890, when control over immigration was given to the federal government, and the U.S Congress appropriated $75,000 to build the first federal immigration station there. Up to April 18, 1890, Castle Garden was used as the immigrant processing center. On that date the United States Treasury took over immigration and moved the processing center to the Barge Office on the Battery at the tip of Manhattan. On January 1, 1892, the immigration station at Ellis Island officially opened.

14

During this transition, immigrants were received at the Barge Office. Over the years, Ellis Island suffered its share of setbacks. First, on June 15, 1897, a fire caused structural damage to the buildings, and while there were no deaths, immigration records of nearly 1.5 million immigrants dating from 1855, were destroyed. The construction of a new, fireproof immigration station soon began, and processing was temporarily transferred back to the Barge Office until Ellis Island reopened on December 17, 1900.

In 1916, Ellis Island suffered additional damage from explosions, supposedly set by German saboteurs, at nearby Black Tom Wharf in New Jersey. The following year, when the United States entered World War I, Ellis Island was used to detain crews from German merchant ships anchored in the New York harbor. As the war progressed, immigration declined, and the U.S. Army and Navy used Ellis Island as a station to treat returning sick and wounded American servicemen. The post-war years brought an influx of immigrants and Ellis Island once again was used as the main station for processing newcomers to America.

In line with approximately 30 other immigrants, Verona and Mary filed into the main building and were directed to the large baggage room in the center of the ground floor. There they were given landing cards, which would help identify them to officials later in the admission process, and they also deposited their luggage. For Verona it was a narrow oak trunk, which contained two or three dresses, a goose-feather quilt, a few family photographs and her prayer book.

Verona and Mary then climbed the staircase to the Great Hall where the medical and legal examinations were conducted. Doctors waiting at the top of the stairs watched them for signs of heavy breathing, limping and physical defects. Once they reached the top the women had to walk in a circle in front of the doctor. Then the doctors examined their hair and faces, looking for signs of contagious diseases. At the first sign of any suspected medical problem, an immigrant would be taken out of line and his clothing marked with blue chalk: "H" for heart disease, "E" for eye problems, and "L" for lameness.

Mary passed the examination without difficulty, but the doctor noticed Verona breathing heavily and she was pulled from the line, given a chalk mark (perhaps a "T" for tuberculosis), and taken to the hospital building across the ferry slip for a full physical examination to determine if she had a contagious disease. The diagnosis of either a contagious disease, or a mental illness were two of the major reasons for denying immigrants admission and sending them back home. Rejection rates during the peak immigration years were only about two percent. Immigrants were supposedly examined thoroughly by the steamship companies at their ports of departure. The steamship companies would be held responsible for the immigrant's return passage and would also be charged about $100 for each person sent back.

In the days that followed, Verona's strength and stamina were evaluated through a series of tests as the doctors checked her for further symptoms of tuberculosis. The test results revealed asthma, a condition my grandmother had had since she was twelve years old. The doctors released her.

Verona then continued through the next stage of the immigration process, the legal examination, which consisted of more than two dozen questions asked in about two minutes. Presumably, the questions had been asked in Europe before the immigrant was sold a steamship ticket; the legal inspectors just re-asked the same questions. The inspectors had the manifest sheets from all the ships in front of them, listing all the passengers who arrived on a given day. Each immigrant wore a manifest tag on his or her clothing with two numbers on it—the page and line on the manifest sheet with the immigrant's name. The answers to the questions were recorded on that sheet beside the immigrant's name. The common practice was for the legal inspector to look an immigrant straight in the eyes as he fired his questions rapidly one after the other "What is your name?" "Where were you born?" "How old are you?" "Where are you coming from?" "Where are you going? With the aid of an interpreter, my grandmother's answers would have been: "Verona Straka." "Presov, Czechoslovakia." "Twenty-two." "Milpos." "Pennsylvania."

On average, each inspector would see 400 to 500 immigrants per day. To this man before her, Verona was just another face. If her answers had seemed the least bit suspicious, she would have been removed from the line once again, and this time an "SI" chalk mark would have been placed on her clothing. "SI" meant the immigrant would be detained and sent before the Board of Special Inquiry.

This time Verona did not receive any marks on her clothing. The inspector, satisfied with Verona's answers, waived her on to be reunited with Mary, who had passed both the medical and legal examinations but remained on Ellis Island in one of the dormitories. For 80 percent of the immigrants, the average stay on Ellis Island was roughly three to five hours. Verona had been detained for approximately seven days.

After Verona received her clearance, the two women exchanged their foreign currency for American money and purchased railroad tickets to Pennsylvania at one of the offices that did business on the island. A ferry took them across the river to New Jersey, where they waited at the depot for the train that would take them to their final destination of Duquesne, Pennsylvania, where Verona's sister, Maria, had settled upon coming to America.

At that time, Duquesne, named for the Governor General Marquis Duquesne of Canada, was a thriving mill town located 12 miles southeast of Pittsburgh on the Monongahela River, and at the southern terminus of the Bessemer and Lake Erie Railroad. Among the first white settlers was Lieutenant John Frazier, who in 1753 lived and traded with Indians at the mouth of Turtle Creek. Historical papers have also speculated that Frazier entertained George Washington in his hut and that Washington passed through Duquesne sometime before his return to Williamsburg in 1754.

In the early part of 1885, the Duquesne Steel Company purchased a tract of farming land along the river front from Robert Patterson and Mrs. Priscilla Kennedy. In the following years, mills were erected by the Allegheny Bessemer Steel Company, the National Tube Works Company of McKeesport, and the Howard Plate Glass Company. In 1889, the Allegheny Bessemer Steel

17

Company sold out to the Carnegie Steel Company, founded by business mogul Andrew Carnegie.

Verona's sister Maria lived in a modest duplex at 129 Crawford Avenue, located approximately one mile from the train station, and Mary and Verona were escorted there by a cantor (choir leader) from St. Peter & Paul Greek Catholic Church, which Maria attended. It was never revealed why Maria settled in Duquesne, but in general immigrants tended to settle in or nearby areas where relatives already lived.

Verona never talked about how she felt when she arrived in Duquesne. But, I imagine that even as a young woman, Verona put her own feelings and worries aside to help Mary adjust, not only to her reunion with the mother she had not seen for 16 years, but also to her mother's husband, Michael Shivak (the only father she would ever know), as well as his three children. At some point, although it is not known when, Mary would come to learn the true identity of her biological father.

The move to Duquesne undoubtedly had great psychological impact on my grandmother and Mary. In the urban industrial centers of America, women who moved from the traditional agricultural villages, such as those in Slovakia, literally faced a new world. First and foremost they had to adjust to an unfamiliar and sometimes hostile physical environment. They were surrounded by unfamiliar food and clothing, as well as a different language, new customs and values.

The way a woman coped with the shock of immigration was often determined by her age, personality and earlier experiences. Those who were young, flexible, adventurous, or physically and emotionally strong adjusted more easily than those who were not. For the vast majority of immigrants, earning a living was the most immediate problem.

Not long after they settled in America, single women like my grandmother and Mary would receive a visit from a representative of the Immigrant Protective League, who would obtain the names of immigrant girls from the various ports of entry. The representative spoke the immigrant's language, and helped him or her adapt to the new environment. Adjusting to life in a new country was difficult at best for any immigrant, especially in terms of being able to secure immediate employment. Ignorant of the English language, the country and the American standard of wages, the immigrant was virtually defenseless in the labor market. The immigrant woman had her own special concerns. Most of them began their new life in America indebted to a relative or friend who had paid for their steamship ticket, as Verona and Mary were to their own mothers.

Often, in circumstances such as my grandmother's, when a girl came to live with a relative, financial responsibility on the part of the relative ended just as soon as the girl found her first job. But finding employment was not always easy; in many cases the women were so young that their only work experience in the old world had been attending to cattle and sheep.

Half of all Slovak women immigrants were employed in service-oriented jobs, most often as domestics. There were not many occupational alternatives available to young, single women at that time. Women in cities dominated by heavy industry, such as Pittsburgh, had fewer opportunities for employment than women in cities like New York or Philadelphia with more diverse economies. Sometimes cultural values restricted employment opportunities as in the case of Southern Italian women who avoided domestic service because it removed them from the protection of their fathers, husbands, or other male relatives. Other times, a woman's ethnic background made her suitable for certain jobs. For example, Slavic women might be hired for jobs in stockyards or foundries because of the stereotype that they were capable of doing work considered physically too heavy for other women. Immigrant women often encountered discrimination based on appearance, age, gender and ethnicity.

Many foreign women were forced to go through an employment agency to find a job, but Verona did not have to go through this process. Her sister recommended her for a job as a housekeeper for a Jewish family in the Squirrel Hill district of Pittsburgh. Once a week, Verona would take the train from Duquesne to clean the family's house. She earned just enough to pay for her own room and board, which cost her about two dollars a month. Mary also found work as a domestic.

Aside from employment concerns, homesickness was nearly a universal problem among all immigrants, especially for women. For most women, coming to the United States meant breaking ties with loved ones for many years, if not forever. The pain of separation was often overwhelming at times. The language barrier often compounded loneliness for those who did not speak English. Surely, Verona and Mary must have felt homesick and disappointed as they adjusted to their new surroundings..

The everyday stresses of life in the city made it a dangerous place in which to live. Poverty and discrimination usually condemned immigrants to the worst, most crowded housing. The house at 129 Crawford was a modest duplex, but a step up from the usual dark, poorly ventilated tenements, which typically housed Slavic immigrants. Certainly, there must have been times when Verona missed the green fields of Milpos. In contrast to the sprawling woods and fresh air of her village, she now endured life in the noisy, smoky and industrialized atmosphere of Duquesne.

Immigrant women coped with the stresses of urban life by drawing on a variety of resources available to them. Family, friends, neighborhoods and churches served as the vehicles to help them adjust to their new environment. Not all women who came to American adjusted successfully. Many were overwhelmed by poverty, loneliness, chronic illness, or insanity. Some died of malnutrition, disease, or complications of pregnancy and childbirth. Some committed suicide. My grandmother was fortunate to have the support of her family, friends, and neighbors, as well as church members to help her with the problems of initial adjustment.

Another way to help alleviate some of the problems, especially loneliness, was through marriage. Because they were single, Verona and Mary were good candidates for matchmaking with single immigrant men. In most instances, a woman did not have a say about whom she married. This was true for Mary, as her mother had selected an eligible husband for her shortly after her arrival. The man was a steelworker named Andrew Yuhasz

20

(Juhász), a boarder in her mother's house. Andrew was born in America, but was of Slovak descent. The couple married in July of 1924, in St. Peter and Paul Greek Catholic Church. Verona was Mary's maid of honor.

There is a photograph of the two women taken on Mary's wedding day. In this photo, the two women look quite different than they did in the earlier photograph of them as young girls growing up in Slovakia. Mary is wearing an ankle length wedding dress with a scoop neck that is intricately woven with fine, white lace. Her hair is cut above her ears, and covered with a veil that flows to the floor and is decorated with a gathering of beads in the front. She has on white stockings and flat white shoes that have straps across instep of the foot. A strand of pearls graces her thin neck. She is holding a large bouquet of roses and carnations, with ribbons dangling from each side. Mary's gown was either part of the traditional dowry prepared for her back in the old country, or sewn by her mother. Verona is attired in a simple three-quarter length dress with a round neckline of some light color fabric, perhaps pink or blue, covered with a thin sheer lace in the front. Verona also wears pearls around her neck and has on stockings and shoes similar in style to Mary's. Verona's dark hair is not pulled back away from her face as it had been in the other picture, but is much shorter and curled under. The girls probably retained the cropped hairstyles meted out to them in Hamburg before they boarded the boat for America. In the photo, Verona is also holding a bouquet of roses, with a single carnation mixed in. Verona is standing slightly behind Mary, and her left arm is interlocked with Mary's right arm.

Once married, Mary and her husband moved into their own home, next door to where her mother lived. Mary and Verona maintained a close relationship, but eventually the time came for Verona to move on and prepare for her own marriage.

On occasion, Verona would visit her other two sisters, Susan Gereg and Katherine Kolcun, who had immigrated many years before and lived in Midway, Ohio. Midway was and remains a small town located a few miles from St. Clairsville, in Belmont County. Verona would take the train from Pittsburgh to St.

Clairsville to Barton and a family member would then escort her, on foot, to one of her sisters' homes. It was during one of these visits that she met her future husband—the man I would eventually come to know as "Grandpap."

CHAPTER THREE
JÁNOŠ

When my grandmother first met Jánoš (John) Figlar, he was a 28-year-old coal miner living with his brother Jacob in Fairpoint, Ohio. Like Verona, he too had immigrated from Czechoslovakia via Ellis Island, arriving 11 months before she did. They met in July of 1924, not long after Mary's wedding. Their meeting was arranged by John Kolcun, the husband of Verona's sister Katherine. Within a few months Jánoš and Verona became engaged.

Jánoš, by all accounts, was a handsome young man. He stood 5'5 and had blue eyes, brown hair, and fair skin. In a photo taken a few years earlier for his passport, he is wearing a suit and tie with a white shirt, the collar tight, almost stiff, against his neck. His hair is combed back from his forehead, drawing attention to his thin mustache, rounded at the ends. In full view, his pointed chin and angled cheek bones. He looks poised and proud, like a figure from a Hollywood movie magazine.

Although he was not very tall (most Slovak men were rather short in stature probably due to a poor diet), Janos possessed a strong and muscular body structure. His masculine face is trimmed with a black mustache, he eyes full of fire, his forehead is free, his behavior self-aware without being impertinent." From the descriptions and photos of Jánoš at this age, he appears to basically fit this description, although he was a bit short in for a Slovak man.

Verona knew little about Jánoš except that he was three years older than she, was of Slavic descent and had a reputation as a hard worker. It was not until many years after they were married that Verona learned of the circumstances which brought this man to America and into her life.

Jánoš was born on March 14, 1896, to Jánoš and Anna Gazdik Figlyár in Osturnja (pronounced O-sturn-ya), or in English, Osturna, a village located in northeastern Slovakia not far from the Polish border. Osturna is known for its mountains, "The High Tatras," visible from the south and southwest and once rich in copper, iron, gold, and silver. Village history dates the founding of Osturna back to the 1500s by Lemko Rusyns, often referred to as Carpatho-Rusyns (KAR-PAY-tho-ROO-sins) or Ruthenians. The Rusyns (once known as White Croats) are said to have settled in the Carpathian Mountain region (of the former Austro-Hungarian) empire during the sixth and seventh centuries A.D. as part of the great Slavic migration during that time. They came from the areas of Galicia and Volhyhia (to the north and east) and Podolia (today known as the Ukraine). Due to the lack of any firm geographic identity, Rusyns have often been referred to as the people from "No Man's Land." My grandfather always referred to himself as a "Slovak." I am not certain whether this was because he did not know he was a Rusyn or because he just chose to identify himself as Slovak.[5]

The Carpatho-Rusyns came from small villages and were, in general, a poor people. The mountainous terrain that surrounded their villages prevented large-scale agricultural production, forcing most Carpatho-Rusyns to make a living through farming, forestry, and shepherding livestock. Their language, an East-Slavic dialect, has been influenced by other languages such as Hungarian, Polish and Slovak influences, and is written in the Cyrillic Alphabet (partly based on Greek letters, and partly on Latin, which was invented by St. Cyril so that the Russian church could show it was separated from both the Roman and Greek churches). In terms of religion, Carpatho-Rusyns generally belonged to the Greek Catholic Church. My grandfather was baptized Greek Catholic and raised in the Carpatho-Rusyn traditions.

In Russian, the name "Figlyar" means "Mountebank," which in English is defined as a "quack doctor, charlatan; any boastful or false pretender." I doubt that Jánoš knew this was the meaning of his name and wonder what he would have made of it had he known. Interestingly, in later years, my grandmother often referred to his family as "a bunch of gypsies."

---

5 Today, Rusyns in Slovakia are undergoing a revival after the fall of Communism in 1989. Under Communism, Rusyns were declared to be Ukrainians and could not have their own cultural institutions nor use their own language; most chose to identify as Slovaks rather than Ukrainians.

Jánoš' family lived in a dwelling that was characteristic of Osturna—a log house asymmetrical in structure, made of dressed timber with small windows, a dirt floor, and a shingled roof. Inside there were three areas: the entrance vestibule, the living room and the pantry, with a stove made of mud and built into the corner of the room. In the back was an outhouse built from timber, and a cattle barn.

Jánoš was the youngest of eleven children. Jánoš ' father, a cabinet-maker, died unexpectedly, when Jánoš was just a young boy. His mother soon remarried, and later moved from Osturna to Podolinec. Jánoš rarely talked about his stepfather, except to say that he did not like him.

As a young man, Jánoš served as an apprentice to a carriage maker. While still learning the trade he went to serve in the Austro-Hungarian army. It was compulsory for all young men to enlist in the army when they reached the age of 21, but for some reason Jánoš joined at 13 and ended up serving for approximately eight years. He was 18 years old when the First World War began. By this time, three of Jánoš' brothers had left their homeland. They were among the 125,000-150,000 Carpatho-Rusyns who arrived in America before 1914. Simeon arrived in America around 1892. Jacob had left Osturna in 1905 to find work in America, and Joseph left in 1910 (presumably as a stowaway) to avoid induction into the military.

Although the outbreak of the war blocked passage out of the country and virtually halted emigration, I do not believe this is the sole reason why Jánoš stayed behind. My mother often referred to him as a man of conviction. She also remembered him talking about having respect for one's country and the importance of loyalty.

During the war, Jánoš spent time in a Russian prison where his ability to repair carriages and make wheels saved his life. Eventually he managed to escape and returned to his homeland on foot in 1920. By that time his mother lived in Podolinec, about 14 miles from Osturna. Soon after his return, Jánoš received letters from Jacob telling of the promise of work in America. This prospect of employment, his dislike for his stepfather, and his own

25

imprisonment helped to entice Jánoš to say good-bye to his mother and siblings and leave home.

On September 8, 1921, with forty-five dollars in his pocket—all that was left after paying for his steamship ticket—Jánoš boarded the S.S. Lapland at Antwerp, Belgium, and after his ship made brief stops at Cherbourg and Southampton sailed for America. Nine days later, he arrived in New York, his name noted as "Jan Figlar" on the passenger arrival list. Once Jánoš settled in America, he changed the spelling of his name to "John Figlar."

All three of Jánoš' brothers had settled in the vicinity of Barton, Ohio, close to the West Virginia border and a chief mining area for bituminous or soft coal. The town drew a large population of Slovak immigrants, many of whom came from Osturna because the hilly terrain of the Ohio Valley and the Wheeling Creek reminded them of their village back in Eastern Europe. Slovaks were traditionally a people with agrarian interests who were bound closely to the soil. Oddly enough, however, many who came to America in the 19th century did not engage in commercial farming in the new world. Owning land was a long-term commitment that they were not prepared to make because their main goal was to earn enough money to some day return to Slovakia and buy land there. Furthermore, these immigrants lacked the capital necessary to buy land or invest in farm animals or machinery.

By the time Jánoš' brothers immigrated in the 20th century, however, the scenario had changed. Many immigrants, including Jánoš' brothers, who apparently did not have any intention of returning to Slovakia, did buy land and engage in farming. Jacob, a coal miner by trade, had purchased a small plot of land in 1912 on the east half of Wheeling Township, leading up Wheeling Creek from Fairpoint near the Pittsburgh #8 Coal Vein. His brother, Joseph, also owned a farm in nearby Bannock, where he lived with his wife, Barbara, and two daughters, Mary and Kitty. The eldest brother, Simeon (who was also called Sam), lived with Joseph for a while, but he was reportedly a bachelor, and was basically a wanderer.

Jánoš stayed with Jacob and his wife, Eva, who were expecting their first child. Following in his brothers' footsteps, as

26

well as those of other Slovak men, Jánoš obtained a job in a nearby coal mine. While immigrants with professional backgrounds often had trouble finding immediate employment in the new world, because of the language barriers, average laborers like Jánoš, with the physical stamina and eagerness to work were able to get jobs. In the early days of immigration, agents enticed young Slovak men to America to work in the mines, mills, coke ovens and foundries, and occasionally even in construction or on the railroads. Mining, in particular, provided quick employment. Once the word spread, and those who were already in America sent evidence of the "easy" money to be earned across the ocean, back to their families and friends, many more Slovaks were drawn to America.

Jánoš and his brothers were enticed. They had been told that Slovak workers were in high demand. Slovak workers were known to be diligent, efficient, honest, capable of working long hours and enduring great physical hardships, and would put in a full day of work for a full day's pay. Sometimes this moral obligation backfired and they were cheated out of their rightful pay by unscrupulous bosses. Despite a boss' dishonesty, great endurance and a notion that they were paid for what they could produce, often caused Slovak men to remain in unskilled laborer positions for long periods of time, some even permanently.

For most immigrants, work came to identify the worker, and an immigrant group's cultural idiosyncrasies tended to define the kind of work he did. Italians, for example, typically worked as public construction workers or builders and tended not to work in mines. For Italians, the nature of their work was peer-oriented: they had a cultural-based need to see and talk to one another. Underground work, which tended to isolate workers from one another was not conducive to socialization and therefore prevented them from associating with their peers. But Slavic men, like Jánoš, could be found laboring underground in the mines. In Slavic culture there was a strong distinction between male and female work. The man did physical labor and tended not to do work that involved food preparation or clothing fabrication and maintenance. Thus, it was not likely for one to see a Slavic man in the garment industry. Slavs also held a basically weak concept of peers in relation to work; for them the purpose of work was to earn money and the security of having a job was the greatest thing they could pass on to their sons.

Jánoš exemplified this picture of a diligent and honest Slavic worker; he did not mind performing menial tasks to earn money. As an unskilled laborer he earned little more than $2.36 per hour, but even so, he fared far better in America than he would have working in the fields back in Slovakia.

It was at the Troll Mining Company that Jánoš met John Kolcun. As a young man, Jánoš desperately wanted to marry, yet he would not settle for just any woman. His prospective bride had to be Slovak, preferably straight from Europe. He was not alone in his desire to marry a woman from the "old country." First-generation Slovaks married fellow Slovaks in overwhelming numbers and were apt to choose spouses from the same, or neighboring, villages.

Aware that Jánoš was in search of a bride, John believed he knew the perfect woman for him. That woman was Verona. Family stories have indicated that the marriage may have even been planned before my grandmother came to America, which has caused me to wonder whether or not my grandmother loved my grandfather. She never expressed her feelings to me or even to her own children. What makes the "arranged" marriage theory seem plausible is a story that my mother once told me about another Slovak girl who was interested in Jánoš, yet he never reciprocated the feelings. The girl remained single for the rest of her life, while Jánoš became betrothed to Verona.

My grandmother would not have been the only immigrant woman to have her husband chosen for her. Even her niece, Mary, married just a few months prior, had experienced such an arrangement. Although the notion of romantic love as the basis for marriage became prevalent in American culture in the 1800s, arranged marriages were still common among the various immigrant groups. Typically parents arranged marriages in order to achieve social or economic advantages. The bride and groom usually played no part in the decision, meeting for the first time at the wedding itself. Traditional practices such as the dowry were established to guarantee a suitable match or to provide insurance against divorce or widowhood by supplying the woman with goods, land or money. The most common form of matchmaking involved the direct approach where the father became friends with the potential groom and talked about his daughter (in her absence) describing her physical charms, character and capacity for companionship, readiness for marriage, health, strength and family training. Sometimes the suitor would agree to forward money for her passage due to the scarcity of women and social barriers of marrying into other nationalities. A father would pledge his daughter to the man and agree to live with newlyweds and maintain their new home.

For those immigrants from Eastern European cultures, matchmaking was almost inevitable. This held true for Slovaks, especially due to the large number of single men who came to America prior to WWI and who eventually wanted wives.

As time went on, many young immigrant women were determined to choose their own husbands without the traditional guidance of their parents. They desired to marry for love as they assumed true Americans did. In reality, however, relatives, friends, co-workers, and even professional matchmakers or advertisements in ethnic newspapers helped women find husbands of the appropriate ethnic background, religion or class. Although marital obligations and gender roles differed according to class, ethnic or religious background, they were generally clearly defined and enforced by family and community.

For Verona, living in a new country failed to fully separate from her Slavic culture and the Eastern European ways still influenced the way she lived her life. In planning for her marriage, love was not a factor. Although in Jánoš, she must have seen stability, the promise of a home and, eventually, a family. Later on in life, whether or not my grandmother believed she ended up with the right person was something she kept to herself.

Nevertheless, the match was made and elaborate preparations began for what would be one of the most momentous events in her life. In fact, the preparation for a Slovak girl's marriage began during infancy. Her mother and grandmothers wove linens and clothing from flax, made household necessities such as towels and grain or potato sacks, and knitted feather quilts that would become part of the girl's dowry. All of these items were put into beautifully painted chests or wardrobes along with other family treasures. This evolved into the Eastern European idea of the "hope chest" to prepare woman for things needed in her own home. A great deal of time and money went into these preparations. Undoubtedly, these things were among those items, which Grandma brought with her when she made the journey to America.

Prior to a couple's engagement, it was customary in Slavic culture for the groom to take his best friend to the home of the potential bride and ask her parents for formal consent to the marriage. Since Verona's parents were so far away, Jánoš went with his best friend, Steven Troyanovich, and asked her sister Susan, with whom Verona now resided in Midway. In keeping with tradition, the couple had a relatively short engagement of approximately three months. On October 14, 1924, at the County Courthouse in St. Clairsville, they applied for their marriage license. During this time Jánoš and Verona also went to the priest at St. Nicholas Greek Catholic Church for instruction and their wedding banns (the announcement in church of a proposed marriage) were made public several weeks before the impending ceremony. The banns served as a declaration of the couple's intent to marry. If any member of the church knew of a reason the couple should not be marry, for example, if one of them was already married, there would be time to cancel the ceremony.

Jánoš and Verona received no objections to their intent to marry and their wedding date was set. They would be married two weeks later—on the first day of November.

CHAPTER FOUR
AN ARRANGED MARRIAGE

As many long-time residents recalled, the Straka-Figlyar nuptials were the talk of the town in Fairpoint in November of 1924. Some seventy years later the wedding was fondly remembered by parishioners of St. Nicholas Greek Catholic Church who either as children attended the affair or whose relatives were in the wedding party. Why this particular wedding should figure so prominently in the minds of those attendees is not clear, but nevertheless, it took just a simple showing of a photograph of the wedding party to elicit memories of an event, which not only joined my grandparents together, but also united the Slavic community of the area.

Out of all the occasions uniting family and community together in the Slavic culture, none matched the joy and festivity of a wedding. Weddings, births and funerals were not only the three most special occasions celebrated in the Slavic community, but they also corresponded to sacraments in the church, namely christenings, marriage, and extreme unction (anointing of the sick or last rites). Such religious feast days represented the expansion (or loss in the case of death) of both the immediate family and the larger parish or church family and involved some type of gathering.

Traditional Slovak wedding ceremonies were complex and still are. Weddings began with a solemn church service and ended with a large reception, usually held in a local hall to accommodate several hundred guests. The celebration could last from two days to two weeks, depending on how much money the bride's parents were willing, or able, to spend. In Slovakia, a typical wedding lasted as long as ten days. In America, the economic and social conditions did not permit such lengthy celebrations. My grandparents' wedding lasted three days and brought together as many of the rich cultural traditions of the old country as the new world would allow.

The festivities began on Friday after the men finished their shifts in the mine. The men gathered at the home of the bridegroom and gave him a traditional scolding. They made jokes and teased him with comments about giving up his bachelor status. The next morning, the guests returned to Jánoš' home and a procession formed. Had they been back in Europe, the procession would have included horse-drawn wagons decorated with brightly colored ribbons. A gypsy would have traveled in the first wagon, followed by the bridegroom, best man and groomsmen in the next wagon, and guests in the remaining wagons. They would have gone to the bride's home and had breakfast with her family. The bride and bridesmaids would then be escorted to the third wagon and the procession then followed to the church. In Fairpoint, they traveled by foot from house to house and took a train between towns.

In Slovakia, the wedding day began when the couple knelt before the parents to formally ask forgiveness for past wrongs and a blessing for the future. Because they were in America, Verona and Jánoš were unable to adhere to this custom; both of their fathers were dead, and their mothers were back in Slovakia and unable to attend the ceremony. Jánoš' brothers and Verona's sisters had to stand in place of their parents. At times like these, Verona must have missed her mother. There was the personal loss of not having her support but also the breaking of tradition: the first in a chain of events, which would separate her from her ethnic heritage.

The marriage ceremony took place at St. Nicholas Greek Catholic Church in Barton, a light colored brick building with a gold dome and three-barred cross—a visible symbol associated with the Greek Catholic religion. Both Jánoš had Verona had been raised according to the traditions of the Greek Catholic Church, so it was proper that they solemnized their wedding vows in that faith. The church held special significance for Jánoš because it resembled the one in Osturna, where he was baptized. Most of the immigrants who founded the church in 1913 came from Osturna and wanted to build a carbon copy of St. Michael's. Among the founders was Jánoš' brother, Joseph Figler.

In the Eastern Church, the sacrament of marriage is referred to as "crowning," a symbolic representation of the union between Christ the King and his Bride (the Holy Church) and a solemn blessing of the man and the woman that their new life together may be one of unity and concord. As bride and groom, Jánoš and Verona were conducted to the middle of the church by the priest, Father Duthovsky, for the "crowning." The priest blessed them three times "O Lord our God, crown them with glory and honor." Crowns were placed on their heads and worn until the end of the service.

Jánoš and Verona then listened to a reading of Ephesians v, 20-23: "Giving thanks always for all things in the name of our Lord Jesus Christ in God the Father. Be subject to one another in the fear of Christ. Let wives be submissive to their husbands as to the Lord; because a husband is head of the wife, just as Christ is head of the Church, being himself savior of the body."

A husband is head of the wife. These words would stay with Verona.

After the recitation of the Lord's Prayer, Jánoš and Verona drank wine from the same cup as a token of their new unity. The priest took them by the hand and led them three times around the lectern while the choir sang. Their participation in the solemn service signified the sanctity of married life—a connection between human love and love of God. In orthodox beliefs when two people marry, they enter into an organic relation, so close that it is not dissolved even by death. Their two lives were now sealed.

After the ceremony, the couple and the wedding party boarded a train for St. Clairsville where a photograph—the one that triggered the memories of some the attendees so many years later—was taken in a local studio. I am fascinated by this surprisingly crisp image. This picture, I later learned, caused hard feelings between my grandfather and his brother, Jacob because Jacob's wife, Eve, wanted their infant daughter to sit between the bride and groom in the picture. Jánoš refused because he thought a baby in between them would cause false speculation about the reason for the marriage. There are thirty-one people in the photograph—all dressed in their Sunday best. The men were attired in plain, dark suits, and the women wore dresses of varied lengths and colors (some white, some dark). Stephen Troyanovich, Jánoš' good friend and fellow coal miner, was the best man. The matron of honor was Helen Zaleta, a friend of Verona's from Pittsburgh. Verona had become close to Helen while working in Pittsburgh and chose her over Mary for this distinction. Although included in the general wedding party photo, Verona's niece, Mary (Straka) Yuhasz, did not play an important role. The other attendants included relatives, and several of Jánoš' co-workers and their wives.

Typically Slovak couples were married in their best clothing. But often, as part of tradition, the groom paid for the bride's wedding garment. The bride would get a new pair of boots for the occasion—after the wedding she seldom put them on again for fear of wearing them out, but would carry them over her shoulder to church or other special occasions to show that she had them and often saved them to be buried in.

Verona's dress was white covered with beads, as was her thin, sheer veil. She wore the ankle-high lace-up boots, and held a bouquet of white carnations in her lap. Jánoš was clean-shaven, his mustache gone. He wore a dark suit, with a carnation pinned to the lapel. The look on his face makes me think he was much happier than Verona.

After the wedding photographs were taken, the *Starosta* (or Master of Ceremonies) escorted Jánoš and Verona to their reception, which was held back in Fairpoint, where the entire street was blocked off for the occasion.

Upon arrival the bride and groom were given wine, bread and salt to eat, symbolizing that the bride would never go hungry. Then the *Starosta*, who was one of Jánoš' older co-workers and a close friend, recited anecdotes about the couple's past and future, making humorous remarks about the groom's way with women and the couple's fertility. In accordance with a special custom associated with Jánoš' Rusyn roots, the couple had their hands tied together with an embroidered scarf and were marched around the kitchen table three times to symbolize unity for life.

34

A ten-course meal followed. Weeks before the event, Verona's sisters began the preparations for the many dishes which lined the tables set up along the street. They served pork, *kolbassi*, sauerkraut, *holupki* (cooked ground meat and rice wrapped in cabbage leaves), *pirohi* (triangular-shaped dough pockets filled with prunes, potatoes or sauerkraut and tossed in browned butter) pickled beets, potatoes, desserts of *kolaci* (cookies) and yeast breads filled or covered with prunes, apricots, or other fruits, crushed nuts or poppyseed. The homemade beer, whiskey, and *slivovica* (a Slovak liquor distilled from plums) or the stronger *palenka* (literally "firewater") was provided by male in-laws and other relatives, partly because of Prohibition, but mostly because it was traditional for Slovaks to make their own liquor. Eating was a continuous affair, often done in shifts. The endless supply of food and drink was something that Andrew Troyanovich, whose father served as best man, fondly remembered. Andy was only five years old when the wedding took place but he remembers going from table to table trying out the different food items that were served.

There was drinking and dancing all night to folk and gypsy music. Slavs were often criticized for their ceremonies, especially their weddings. Such gatherings were generally frowned upon by outsiders, particularly by the more conservative Protestants, who considered them demonstrations of a barbarian culture. Regardless of the criticism, such methods for celebration continued in the Slavic community and were passed down through the generations. This was true for my own family as well.

Jánoš and Verona danced the traditional Slovak dances. First there was the usual two-step polka, and also the *cardas* (char-dush) where the woman places her hands on the man's shoulders and the man places his hands on each side of her waist, and the two move two steps to the right, two steps to the left in time with the music. As the tempo of the music changed to a fast beat, the couples would twirl around as the man would raise one arm and shout, "hey, hey." Jánoš loved to participate in these traditional dances and was quite good at them.

They also had a bridal dance (*redovy*), where the bride danced with male guests for a fee. In Carpatho-Rusyn tradition, it is typically the last dance of the wedding. A traditional bridal dance song is played, with some 120 verses and a number of variations depending on one's village and family. During this dance, a man's hat was put on the floor and any man who wanted to dance with the bride put money in the hat. The man then received a drink of whiskey. The bridal dance evolved from the Eastern European custom that required a bride's dance partners to contribute to her dowry. Although the practice of the dowry was generally not carried over from the homeland, the money collected went toward food and drink to keep the party going, and the couple got to keep what was left.

A high point of the celebration was reached toward the end of the evening when a mock hunt for the bride was organized. The bride would hide for the occasion, which symbolized a change of heart and her reluctance to settle down with her new husband. This mock hunt also represented an earlier form of bride purchase when there was a shortage of women among early nomadic peoples. Once the bride was found, she was brought to the women for the traditional capping ceremony.

As midnight approached, the women banished the groom from the hall and the bridesmaids would unveil the *mlada* (bride) and sing sad songs "*Nasa mladajak sosna...*"Our maiden has sprouted like a pine," while the maid-of-honor folded the veil. The master of ceremonies would take the bride's veil and hold it up in the air on a cane and dance around with it during the singing, offering it to the highest bidder. In the old country the bride's wreath or crown was ceremoniously removed by the village matron and replaced with a white, starched *cepec* (cap or kerchief) to be worn at all times, while the bridesmaids continued singing, "no more can she wear ribbons in her hair, but has to wear it rolled up." This was a symbolic transition from maiden to wife. There was an old Slovak myth that hair was magical and had to be concealed once married. The function of the cap in public was that it was a visible sign to show that the woman was married and no longer available for courting. This ceremony was marked with sadness because from then on a woman's life would be greatly constrained: She would work in the home, bear children, and be under the authority of her husband, and often her mother-in-law. I remember how my grandmother always had her hair covered with either a scarf in the winter, or a kerchief in warmer weather, regardless of whether she was indoors or out.

In Slovak villages, the bride and groom usually left for his parents' home after this ritual, but family and guests kept the celebration going. Since they were in America, Jánoš most likely took his bride to his brother's house for their wedding night, while the festivities of their reception continued.

Like many other women of her generation, Verona probably knew little, if anything, about sex. Most did not know about sex until they got married and some young girls did not even know what menstruation was until they had a period. In the era in which Verona grew up mothers did not talk about these things with their young daughters. Verona had been brought up in a very modest family atmosphere, and my great-grandmother was so religious that she probably thought it immoral to discuss such topics. But on her wedding night Verona was no longer a girl.

"No more could she wear ribbons in her hair."

After the wedding, Jánoš and Verona settled into married life in Midway, where he continued to work in the coal mine.

Not long after, Verona told Jánoš that he was going to be a father.

CHAPTER FIVE
MOTHER

Verona spent her first winter in Midway as a pregnant young wife. With this role she assumed her full share of the duties of married life. Her youth gone, she was now subject to the dictates of her husband who was the head of the house. In Europe, the traditional Slavic family was patriarchal, with women held in low esteem. A new bride typically moved into her husband's home and was subject to the authority of her mother-in-law. The only ways a Slavic woman could achieve status was through her dowry, her children, or her husband's position. In the United States, however, a young married Slovak woman's position was immediately higher since she was the manager of her own household and not dependent on her in-laws.

As was the case for most Slavic immigrants, Jánoš and Verona were forced by his low wage to find the cheapest housing possible. They rented a typical three-room, light beige bungalow on Route #2 that had a water pump and outhouse located in back. Verona's sisters, Katherine and Susan, lived within walking distance.

Verona's workdays started early and ended late. She rose before dawn to stoke the coal in the stove that heated the house. She prepared breakfast for her husband and packed his lunch pail with leftovers from supper the day before, and some water or coffee. Since they did not have an indoor toilet, she would have to empty the slop buckets from the previous night into the outhouse.

Once Jánoš left for work, Verona continued with her own tasks. She had to shop almost daily, since there was no refrigeration, and ice was not readily available. She would walk the few blocks to the Midway store to purchase the cheapest cuts of meat (usually pork), milk and other staples. The items were purchased on credit, with the money deducted out of Jánoš' weekly paycheck. Several times a week Verona would bake bread; it was cheaper than paying nine cents a loaf at the store. Since both of

38

her sisters had gardens, she was able to get her vegetables from them.

Typically Monday was known as "wash day" and this was when Verona did the laundry. She boiled the clothes on top of the stove in a copper kettle and lifted them out with a wooden stick. She then scrubbed the garments by hand on a tin washboard, with soap homemade from lye, or with commercial Octagon or Felsnaphtha soap, if she and Jánoš could afford it. With her fingers already red and raw from the coarse soap and hot water, Verona then wrung the clothes by hand and spread them out on the grass or threw them over a fence to dry, and emptied the soapy water into the yard or nearest ditch. Often she had to repeat the process, especially with Jánoš' work clothes, usually heavily soiled with the coal dust and dirt from the mine. Once the clothes had dried, ironing was done on the kitchen table, with a heavy iron heated on top of the stove. Those garments that needed patching or mending were done so by hand. In addition to cooking, laundry, and scrubbing floors, Verona had the extra chore of scouring her iron stovetop which she did with rough-edged bricks—the only cleaning tools at her disposal.

Slavic homes usually varied in cleanliness, depending on the part of Europe from which its inhabitants came, the length of residence in America and the natural habits of the family. From what I know of my grandmother, she was always concerned with having a clean home and worked hard to do so. This was an obsession she eventually passed on to her children.

After the house had been cleaned, Verona prepared for Jánoš' arrival from work. The evening meal was always ready before he walked into the house, and a wooden tub was filled with warm water. Before supper, Verona would scrub the grime and sweat off of her husband's back.

Her only rest came on Sunday mornings, when she and her sisters would take the train into Barton for mass at St. Nicholas. It was important to Verona that she carry on the religious values her mother taught her as a young girl. Going to church also provided a way to socialize with other Slavic women, both after the service and at other times, such as when the women would gather to prepare foods for special church meetings, picnics, weddings or funerals. In the old country, the social life of the Slavic woman almost always involved her neighbors. Once in America, Slovaks tried to have a similar type of social life, but the hours both men and women spent working made this practically impossible. This seemed to be the case more so for women than men. The men at least had the neighborhood bars or taverns and their local ethnic clubs, sports groups or fraternal lodges, such as the National Slovak Society established in 1890. For women, the church was the typical place to meet, but Slovak women eventually rebelled from the male-dominated social organizations and founded their own societies, such as *Živena* and *Ženská Jednota* (The First Catholic Ladies Association).

In addition to caring for a new home and handling the duties of married life, Verona was faced with the impending responsibility of motherhood. For immigrant women beginning a family carried special significance, helping to heal the wound of separation from parents and loved ones left behind. Children also represented the beginning of permanency in America.

Anna, my mother, was born on July 6, 1925. She was named for her paternal grandmother. The local physician, Dr. Martin, delivered the baby, who had green eyes and dark brown hair, at 7:30 in the morning. The doctor must have misunderstood my grandparents' broken English as they gave him the baby's name, and mistakenly filed the baby's name as "Amy" on her birth certificate, instead of "Anna." The mistake went unnoticed by Jánoš and Verona until they went to enroll their daughter in primary school and the officials doing the paperwork discovered the mistake, and required them to file for a corrected certificate.

Twenty days after Anna's birth, Jánoš and Verona gathered with their family and friends at St. Nicholas Church for their daughter's christening. In Slavic culture, christenings, like weddings, marked the expansion of both the family and the parish and involved elaborate celebration. The godparents were carefully selected, with both friendship and financial standing in mind, as they would be responsible for caring for the child in the event of the parents' death and seeing that the child had a Christian upbringing.

My mother's godparents were Helen Zaleta and Andrew Yuhasz (Juhász). Helen, who had served as the matron of Honor at Verona's wedding, was still a close and trusted friend of Verona's, and Andrew, the husband of her niece Mary, was considered financially stable with his job in the steel mill. My mother's baptism involved immersion three times into consecrated water while the Reverend Girecki gave a blessing. In the Greek Catholic Rite, the Mystery of Holy Chrismation or Confirmation follows immediately after baptism. It differs from Confirmation in the Western church in that it is not a renewal of baptismal vows, but a lay ordination where the Christian receives a special grace to participate in the dispensing of all other sacraments.

After the service, the family, godparents, and friends went back to the Figlar home to take part in a feast similar to that shared at their wedding reception. They enjoyed several courses of food, plenty of liquor and celebrated the occasion with music and dancing.

When my mother was 16 months old, she and her parents left Midway. The mines had shut down due to strikes and a poor demand for bituminous coal, and work was scarce. Some men took to farming to earn a living until the mines started working again. Others, like Jánoš, searched elsewhere for mining work. Rather than rely on assistance from the Red Cross or Quaker relief as other unemployed miners were forced to do, Jánoš decided to leave the area. In November of 1926, he packed their belongings and with his wife, who was five months pregnant with their second child, and daughter, moved by train to Wilkes-Barré in northeastern Pennsylvania.

Wilkes-Barre is located on the northern branch of the Susquehanna River, about 100 miles north-northwest of Philadelphia and at one time among the richest anthracite or "hard coal" regions in the world. This 4.8 square mile area is the county seat of Luzerne County, and was one of several towns, including Hazelton, Jessup, Nanticoke, Pittston, and Plymouth where great

41

numbers of Slovaks settled and established significant Slovak communities.

In 1926, the year Jánoš and his family arrived in Wilkes-Barré, the total production of anthracite was about 78 million tons. This was a decline from previous years, when strikes among anthracite mine workers affected production. Nevertheless, when Jánoš moved his family to Wilkes-Barré, the threat of impending strikes failed to hurt his chances of finding a job. Coal was what he came looking for, coal was what he found.

The Lehigh & Wilkes-Barré Coal Company had collieries throughout the region. Jánoš heard of the opportunity for work there through Verona's sister, Sophie Shuga, whose husband worked on the railroad in Wilkes-Barré.

Although the work was more strenuous and the wages a bit better, living conditions remained basically the same as they had been in Ohio. The anthracite miners tended to dwell in small communities known as "Mine Patches" that were owned by the coal company and usually associated with some anthracite colliery. The houses in a mine patch were simply constructed either in long rows as single dwelling homes or as two-, three- and four-family tenements, enclosed by a wooden fence.

Jánoš and Verona rented one of these multi-family tenements on North Walnut Street for $13.50 per month. Verona had a small, sparsely furnished kitchen with a table and chairs, a kerosene lamp, a cabinet for dishes, and a tiny sink, which came with the place, and her sewing machine. In the corner was a coal stove, which Verona used for cooking and for heating the house in winter. There was no icebox or running water. Any water needed for cooking or washing had to be obtained from a communal hydrant outside.

Every morning the loud steam whistle of the colliery sounded as early as 5:00 a.m. to arouse the miners. As Verona prepared her husband's lunch pail, he would dress for work. First, he would pull a pair of dark coveralls over a dark workshirt and over his stocky, 5'5", 150 lb. frame. Then he would put on a black canvas cap that had an electric lamp attached in front, with a wire connected to a battery secured to his belt. Finally, he would put on a jacket or raincoat and rubber boots. As Verona watched her husband walk out the door, I imagine that thoughts of whether or not he would come back to her that evening must have crossed her mind.

For at least eight hours Jánoš labored in the darkness, drilling coal in a coal chamber, with little illumination and poor ventilation for the damp, smoky air. The dangers and catastrophes Verona might have envisioned were real. Every minute her husband had to be on guard for possible suffocation or carbon monoxide poisoning, cave-ins, fires, and explosions.

A whistle at the colliery would alert workers and local residents of disasters. Verona dreaded hearing it. At the end of the day as she spotted Jánoš walking up the road, his body hunched over after working in a cramped space underground all day and a coagulated mass of sweat and dust covering his clothing, Verona must have felt relieved. She had one child to care for and another on the way, and the thought of being widowed loomed over her constantly like a large black cloud.

But whatever fears she may have had, Verona kept them to herself and did not dare to suggest to her husband that he find another occupation. Her responsibility was that of wife and mother and nothing more.

On March 22, 1927, she gave birth to her second child and first son, who was named John, Jr. While my mother was the first-born, the fact that Jánoš now had a son surely must have made him proud. In Slovak villages, sons were valued more highly than daughters. Daughters were considered expensive because when they were old enough to marry, the cost of the wedding was borne by the bride's father, as was the dowry, which often represented the value of a whole house. Thus, the father-to-be hoped to have a son instead of a daughter. In keeping with tradition, Jánoš most likely celebrated the news of his newborn son by buying drinks for his buddies at the neighborhood tavern where the miners gathered after their shifts ended.

The couple's joy over the birth of the baby was tempered by the reality of the local employment conditions. By that time, trouble had surfaced among the three large mining centers of

Pittston, Scranton and Wilkes-Barré in Sprawling District 1, which made up the Wyoming-Lackawanna field. After the strike in 1926, coal production had gradually declined, and the coal industry was unable to recover its markets. Battles between the United Mine Workers—the union to which Jánoš belonged—and the owners ensued. Layoffs, political fighting between union and non-union/ex-union members, and the pursuit of the contract mining system in which the operators leased their mines to independent contractors who were paid by the companies based on the tonnage of coal delivered, contributed to the unrest. Under the contractors, miners were pushed to produce as much coal as they could, despite cutbacks on equipment and safety practices. The contractors also were notorious for cheating on wages and for firing workers who could not produce. Although workers opposed the contract system and the union fought against it, they were unsuccessful in having it eliminated. Jánoš was a believer in worker solidarity and supported the Union, despite the risks involved. The risks were unmistakably real. The company held a monopoly on the mining communities by controlling the jobs, the homes, the land, the taverns and the company store, as well as exercising its influence over the police, sheriff, court and individuals in other high-power positions. A common man, like Jánoš, could not ignore the power of the company.

During the next two years, many collieries converted to part-time operations or were closed down completely and abandoned. Times were getting worse for miners, and Verona, pregnant for the third time did not know from one day to the next whether her husband would have a job. After the birth of Joseph, on April 6, 1929, the inevitable happened. The mine where Jánoš worked shut down, and once again the family was forced to move.

CHAPTER SIX
SETTLING IN A STEELTOWN

My mother's first recollections of her childhood began at about age five—after the family had moved from Wilkes-Barre to Western Pennsylvania. The Stock Market Crash of 1929 was followed by an economic depression—a crisis with worldwide effects, but one more immediately felt by individual families trying to maintain a decent daily existence.

A desperate Verona encouraged her husband to move to Duquesne, where she had lived before they met and where she still had family. Her sister, Katherine, had since left Barton, Ohio, and now with her husband and five children lived in a two-story house in the Polish Hill section of Duquesne. John Kolcun worked in the merchant mill of the Duquesne Works, a plant with steel furnaces and rolling mills built in 1889 on farmland adjacent to the Monongahela River. The Duquesne plant was one of the core mills in Andrew Carnegie's steel empire from the time he acquired it in 1890 until 1901 when he sold his interests to J.P. Morgan to form United States Steel. Verona hoped that John could help Jánoš find a job there.

Duquesne was a different environment from the small town of Midway and the mining patch of Wilkes-Barre. After all, it was a suburb of the larger city of Pittsburgh. As the steel industry expanded, Pittsburgh emerged at the forefront of industrial and urban development. By 1910 the city was already heavily industrialized and led the nation in manufactured products. The work environment was shaped by heavy industry and immigrants were able to find jobs. The steel industry also came to dominate the river community of Duquesne and attracted immigrant laborers.

When immigrants arrived in Pittsburgh, they tended to settle close to others from the same parts of Europe. During the industrial era, ethnic neighborhoods developed in both the city of Pittsburgh and its outlying towns. The topography of the city— hilly terrain and deep hollows—encouraged ethnic concentration because they formed natural boundaries, which separated one area from another. Slavs, along with immigrant groups such as Italians and Jews, formed their own enclaves that encouraged the maintenance of traditional culture and promoted associations between individuals of similar backgrounds through attendance of ethnic churches and partic ipation in community celebrations. Such associations helped to ease the transition for immigrants, used to a rural life in Europe, to city life in America. For example, Italian neighborhoods were located mostly in the northeastern sections of the city, while the Jewish immigrants settled originally in the Hill district (an area that extends from downtown Pittsburgh two miles to the east) and later, moved eastward to Oakland, East Liberty and Squirrel Hill. Slavic immigrants, however, established ethnic neighborhoods in the South Side section, and in mining and steel-manufacturing towns to the east and west of the city. One such town was Homestead, located five miles east of downtown Pittsburgh on the south bank of the Monongahela River, and several miles beyond Homestead, Duquesne.

When Jánoš and Verona arrived in Duquesne with their three children, her sister's crowded five-room, two-story house became even more cramped. Katherine and her husband had five children of their own. But they were family, and for Slovaks, family life generally remained closely knit. As would have been the case in Slovakia, the first two generations often lived together in America, and their boarders were often relatives or friends from their own or neighboring villages. Thus, it was quite natural for Verona to turn to her sister during this time of hardship.

Jánoš was unable to turn to his own family. By the time he moved to Duquesne, two of his three brothers had died. According to family stories, his eldest brother, Simeon (also called Sam), a heavy drinker, froze to death alongside a road in Fairpoint and because he supposedly had no wife or immediate family was buried in a pauper's grave. His other brother, Joseph, had been killed several years earlier in a mining accident. The third brother, Jacob had sold his property in Fairpoint a few years earlier and moved to Cleveland, but Jánoš was too proud to ask him for help.

While the idea of depending on Verona's family gnawed at him, he simply did not have a choice. Had it not been for Verona's relatives, the five of them could have easily ended up living in an abandoned mine or deserted coke oven, as so many displaced miners who found themselves without a job or a home were forced to do.

Jánoš had some savings in the bank, but during that first year they mainly relied on the generosity of Verona's sister for their food and housing. The Kolcuns had a small farm where they raised cows, chickens, geese and pigs in their backyard (at that time there were no city ordinances to forbid the keeping of livestock), which they slaughtered and hung in a smokehouse. They also had apple and cherry trees, grape vines, and a garden.

My mother recalled how my grandfather made weekly trips, walking the five miles to and from the Duquesne mill to look for work, but even with his brother-in-law's help was unsuccessful. He would go to the Social Services department and plead with the social worker in charge to help him secure a job. But there were no jobs to be found and few that were available to an immigrant like Jánoš who only had the equivalent of a fourth grade education. Plus there were many other immigrants in a similar position: In 1930 there were some 5,000 foreign-born white residents in Duquesne. Jánoš would come home cursing in Slovak about the "damn system" and other things my mother did not yet understand. Verona watched her husband's confidence being undermined week after week. It was a terrible blow to the morale and self-respect of a man who was by nature a hard worker, willing to sell his labor for even the smallest wage, if only he could find a purchaser. Despite the rejections, he kept up his energy and initiative and persisted in his search for employment. As a young girl, my mother did not understand what was happening with her parents; she only knew that they were living in a different place now.

I have one photograph of my mother as a young girl. It is a picture of her and her brother John, taken in Ohio, during a visit with their Uncle Joseph's family. She was four years old, and John, Jr. was two. In the photo, they are standing on the porch of their uncle's house. Mother was wearing a white cotton dress with bloomers underneath and white leotards, and tiny black lace-up boots. Her dark hair fell almost to her shoulders, but curled at the ends and was tied with a bow. She is smiling and posed, touching her hair with her left hand and her right hand grasping her dress. John, Jr. is about three inches shorter and dressed in a romper also with thick white leotards and black boots. His blond hair is cropped above the ears and combed in a part to the side. There is an innocence reflected in this photograph of a sister and brother playing outside, not cognizant of life's tragedies surrounding them, such as the tragic death of their uncle, or the ensuing period of economic crisis during which they would grow up.

My mother fondly remembered the first year of living in her Aunt Katherine's house and the times spent with her younger brothers and her cousins. She was particularly close to Mary, who was a few months older than she. In the nice weather, they played the back yard amongst the trees and animals. The boys played games like "Kick the Can" or stick ball, and the two girls jumped rope or played jacks. Anna was petrified of the geese because they honked loudly and ran after her. She would hide behind Mary for protection. Mary was not as shy or fearful as Anna and helped to calm her down when the animals frightened her. From that age on, the two girls developed a friendship that would carry into adulthood.

When Anna was six years old, her mother was again pregnant. Five months later, on January 6, 1931, Verona gave birth to a girl, whom they named Mary, after Verona's mother. Two weeks later, the baby died from complications of pneumonia. Besides birth and marriage, a funeral was the other occasion in which Slovaks came together in large numbers. Out of the three, a funeral outwardly displayed solidarity in the Slovak community the most. Following Slovak custom, the baby was washed by the older women, wrapped in white cloth and laid out at home in the corner of the living room, in a small pine coffin that had been built by male relatives. For three days a black veil hung outside near the door of the Kolcun household as family and friends came by to pay their respects and console Verona. The women brought covered dishes of warm food for the family and took care of the daily chores. Verona kept a prayer vigil over her dead child, accepting the death as God's will. Young Anna held her cousin Mary's hand and the two girls sat in silence near the coffin.

The baby Mary was buried on the third day after a procession and funeral mass at St. Peter & Paul Greek Catholic church. The tearful farewell song "Eternal Memory," or *V'icnaja pamjat*, was sung, and the pine box placed in the cold ground. After the burial, the family and all who came to express their condolences went back to the home for a feast prepared by relatives and neighbors. As a sign of continued mourning, it was often customary for female relatives to wear black for up to one year following a death.

Although in time, life eventually moved on.

*My great-grandmother,
Maria Verbovsky Sztraka.*

*My grandmother's brother, Istvan Straka
(born 1894), a military man who
stayed in Slovakia.*

*My grandmother Verona Straka (left)
and her niece, Mary Straka (right) c.
1922 before leaving Slovakia for
America.*

*Wedding photograph of my
grandparents, Verona Straka
and Jánoš Figlyar,
November 1, 1924.*

*Wedding photograph of my mother and
father, Anna Figlar and John Alzo,
October 14, 1947.*

*My grandfather, Jánoš Figlar
(John Figlar) c. 1921.*

51

CHAPTER SEVEN
GROWING UP SLOVAK-AMERICAN

Eight months after her baby sister's death, Anna entered the first grade at Kennedy School, located on Sixth Street, several blocks from the Kolcuns' house on Elmore Avenue. She used to walk there and back with her cousins Mary, Andy and Nicholas. Anna's brothers, John and Joe, were too young yet to attend.

For immigrants in general, the matter of education was a new concept. In America, education was compulsory and there was a choice between public and parochial schooling. Many Slavic parents viewed the public school as an enemy, objecting to what they presumed was an emphasis on materialism and "American ways" and condemned public education for "antireligious" teachings. Many immigrant parents also had bitter memories of the public school in Slovakia where Hungarian officials tried to eradicate their Slovak culture and turn them into Magyars. Such deep contempt kept some parents from seeing the benefits to be gained for their children through a public education. As a result, this drove many Slovaks to support parochial schools staffed by the priests and nuns of the local ethnic church in an effort to assure their children received instruction in the values and traditions they cherished. Only those children who attended parochial schools were taught in the Slovak language. In parochial schools, the day began around 8:00 a.m. with mass during which children would kneel facing the altar. During the school day, children were taught the same courses as those who went to public school: reading writing, arithmetic, art, geography and social studies. On Friday afternoons, however, nuns taught Slovak language, history and songs.

Slovak Greek Catholic children usually attended Greek or Roman Catholic parochial schools or went to public school. St. Peter & Paul did not have its own school, and as my mother remembered, only children who belonged to the Roman Catholic churches in Duquesne were permitted to attend the Roman

Catholic school, so she went to the Kennedy school, a public school.

In general, the majority of Slavic immigrants had difficulty accepting the common notion that education opened the way to quick advancement in the world. They believed that in school children learned the necessary skills to survive in society, but that once these were learned it was time to leave.

Jánoš , however, was an advocate for his children's public education, although he himself had completed only the fourth grade in Czechoslovakia. He quickly learned English through listening to others speak it at work and taking free classes at night, and could solve just about any math problem. Education was almost an obsession to him, and starting with Anna, he took an avid interest in his children's performance in school, pushing them to study and receive good grades. Verona saw to it that her children went to school and were on time, but when it came to following the monthly report card system, she was at a loss, so she left this task to her husband.

In school, Anna learned English. She remembers many of her Slovak classmates had difficulty learning English because their parents spoke only Slovak at home and initially discouraged the children from speaking anything but their native tongue for fear of breaking with the old ways or having their children know more than they did. But because her father also read and spoke English himself, and pushed his wife to learn, he did not object to Anna learning the language.

While in school, Anna also became aware of the various ethnic backgrounds of her classmates. There were fellow Slovaks with whom she identified, but also children of English, Irish, German and Hungarian descent. Typically, those from English, Irish and German families tended to wear nicer clothes and formed their own cliques. In many instances, these children were the sons and daughters of their parents' bosses—the mill foremen or other prominent citizens. She often found it difficult to make friends with these children who often looked down on them or referred to them as "hunkies," so she and Mary made friends with children from similar Slavic backgrounds.

After she finished the first grade, the family moved out of the Kolcun's house because it was not big enough for all its occupants. This time they went to live with Verona's other sister, Maria Shivak, whom the children called "Aunt Mary." Although now widowed, she lived in the same house at 129 Crawford Avenue. When he was working in Wilke-Barre, Jánoš had helped Maria financially, and to repay her debt, she permitted the family to live with her rent-free. Her stepson, Andy, also lived in the house, as did two or three boarders.

In those days, the taking in of boarders was a common practice among Slovak women, one of the key means available to them to earn extra money. The boarders were usually unmarried Slovak men who worked in the mills. In addition to giving them a place to sleep, Maria washed her boarders' clothes, prepared their breakfast of bread and coffee, packed their lunch buckets and had a hot meal waiting for them when they came home after their shifts ended. For these services the men paid her about three dollars a month. While Maria did all of the food shopping herself, the total food bill was divided among the boarders living in the house. Meat was a separate item. Each boarder paid for his own cuts, which Maria purchased from the butcher for the evening meals. To keep track of whose cut was whose at suppertime, she tied a different color cord around each piece.

Maria's family and the boarders occupied the upstairs of the house. It was typical for lodgers to be given the best sleeping room, so Verona and her family had to live mainly in two basement rooms of the home. The living area consisted of a huge kitchen with only a cabinet for dishes, a table and chairs, a gas powered hot plate, and the black coal stove. There was also a studio couch that pulled out into a bed where she and Jánoš slept. Off the kitchen was a small pantry, which also doubled as a laundry room. Beyond the kitchen was a small room containing the coal furnace. The family did not own a refrigerator. Instead they had an icebox and would place a sign in the window for the iceman that said "25 lb. or 50 lb.," depending on how much was needed.

Due to the limited space in the basement, the children slept in an upstairs bedroom on three beds placed side by side, and were only allowed in the upstairs bathroom at night. During the day they used the toilet in the furnace room. Aunt Mary's bathtub was completely off limits. Instead, Verona bathed the children every Saturday evening in an aluminum tub, one after the other, to save water and soap. Verona also feared that her children might destroy her sister's furniture and other belongings. It was a time of extreme hardship and Verona, through her frugal ways, was careful not to cause any ill feelings between herself and her sister.

Beyond the monetary concerns, Verona worried about the type of moral influence the boarders would have on her young children. Typically in households with boarders, the potential for immoral behavior existed. After all, the boarders were single men with normal sexual desires. In some homes, immoral situations occurred which resulted in broken families. In addition, the overcrowding, especially of washing facilities, often resulted in problems with cleanliness and occasionally the spreading of disease. Fortunately, the boarders living in Maria's home did not cause any trouble, and despite their living situation, Verona saw to it that her children had a religious upbringing, went to mass every Sunday, and followed the teachings of the Greek Catholic Church.

Anna started second grade at the Crawford School, which was only a block away from where they now lived. She no longer had her cousin Mary as a traveling companion and walked to and from school by herself until her brothers became old enough to go. Her memories of life during that time included those of a father out of work and a mother who learned to "make do" as most women did during that period. The phrase "to make do" is an old fashioned way of saying "do the best with what you have," and during the 1930s it became more of a philosophy, and for women like my grandmother, the standard way of life.

As the Depression loomed on, János still could not find employment. For three years, he had tried to find a job without success. The Depression struck the Pittsburgh area and its workers hard. Employment and production in the steel industry declined drastically. By 1932, almost one-third of the total workforce was out of work (approximately 12 million people total and about 3 million women).

Despite the family's bleak financial situation, Verona found herself pregnant again and their third son, Michael, was born on November 6, 1932.

That same month, the presidential election saw incumbent Herbert Hoover fall in defeat to Democratic candidate Franklin D. Roosevelt. Throughout his campaign, Roosevelt had promised an energetic economic policy, which he himself termed the "New Deal." Anna and her family, like other Americans, were anxious for him to make good on his promise.

By the next year, President Roosevelt's first phase of the "New Deal" was under way. While the initial program focused on agricultural subsidies, price and wage control, public works, and improvement of regional structures such as bridges, it accomplished little in the fight against unemployment. Men like Jánoš pleaded for the chance to earn enough money so that they could at least bring some milk and bread into the home.

Since her husband was not successful in finding a job, Verona went to work to support the family. Her employment options were limited, as Pittsburgh was not the most favorable of places for women during the early part of the 20th century. While industry created a large demand for the goods and services produced by men, there was little room in the labor force for women. Shortly after Michael's birth, she found a job cleaning houses. The woman she had worked for in Squirrel Hill prior to her marriage heard that she was once again living in Duquesne and hired her back. Once a week Verona would take the train to Squirrel Hill, leaving her four children in the care of her sister while her husband went out to search for work. In general, families that hired Slovak women for housekeeping appreciated their diligence, loyalty and cleanliness, and spoke of them with high praise. This held true for Verona and upon this woman's recommendation she later found a job as a housekeeper for the superintendent of the Duquesne Schools. This particular job had a bonus for Verona as the superintendent let her take home used or broken toys that the school no longer wanted, such as a baby doll for Anna or a wagon for the boys.

The Depression dampened the hopes of many immigrant women like Verona and restricted their expectations for their children. They did what they had to do to survive. There were hundreds of stories like these. Verona carried a double load trying to earn a living while she cared for an unemployed husband and her young children. Verona, like other immigrant women, followed the restricted avenues open to her and took charge of her life. Through it all, Verona never sacrificed caring for her children. While Verona was never overly affectionate with her children, she was always there for them when they came home from school, or when they needed her. Anna, especially, felt close to her mother. She knew her mother had a great love for her and her siblings, and that she wanted good for all of them.

Verona worked for about two years until she again became pregnant. As Jánoš was still jobless, the family like countless others, was forced to go on relief for about a year. They received about $10 per month for groceries, and Verona receive staples, such as flour, oleo, rice and beans given out by the government during the Depression and distributed at the Duquesne Library. At Christmas, Anna stood in long lines at the library waiting for her small box of hard tack candy that Mayor James Crawford gave out as a treat to all the children in Duquesne.

Verona could only afford the basics when it came to groceries, which she bought on credit at Vezdels or Dudnaks, two of the neighborhood corner stores. These local stores carried limited supplies of meat and vegetables at an expensive price and most of the time the family did without such foods. The children watched inquisitively as their mother made wholesome meals out of the most basic ingredients. A frugal Verona made chicken or vegetable soup quite often, since soup bones were given out for free at that time, and baked bread just about every day. For lunch she would fry "Jumbo" (bologna) and eggs, which the children would have with her homemade bread, baked beans, and milk, if available. When finances hit bottom, they would settle for ketchup on bread.

Free clothes were distributed on occasion to people who stood in line at the public library. They could also visit the Salvation Army to buy dresses and blankets. My mother also remembers wearing second-hand dresses that her mother sewed out of scraps of material from families whose children had outgrown their clothes. For my grandfather, accepting charity was demeaning—a tremendous blow to his ego, but they had no other choice; there were now five children, with the arrival of Helen on January 10, 1935.

By that time, the second phase of the "New Deal" was under way. This phase emphasized social policy and focused on creating employment, improving the social security system, and strengthening the interests of workers, and was the part of the "New Deal" which helped working-class families the most. Along these lines, the Works Progress Administration was established in 1935 to help the country cope with unemployment (more than 1/3 were unemployed during this year) created by the Depression. The WPA (later, in 1939, it became known as the Work Projects Administration) was responsible for the building or improvement of roads, airports, sewage lines and the construction of parks, playgrounds, irrigation systems, and tunnels. Anna recalls her father working on WPA for two years, performing menial tasks such as shoveling snow on bridges in the winter or repairing roads in the milder weather. For such assignments he earned about $9 a day. It was not the job he had been searching for, but it brought in a source of income the family desperately needed. With Jánoš' check from WPA, she made sure to pay her grocery bill each month, and the children would fight over the small bag of candy the shopkeeper would give them as a treat.

It was during this time that Anna entered the sixth grade. She had to change schools because only grades one through five were taught at the Crawford School. The convenience of the Crawford School, only a block away now gone, she had to walk 15 minutes to and from the Libengood School on Sixth Street, which happened to be next to the Kennedy School where she attended First grade. She left the house at 8:00 a.m. each day, came home for an hour at lunch time and returned from school in the afternoon around 4 o'clock with her brother, John, now in the fifth grade, in tow.

After chores, homework and supper, the children would play outside in the small yard or in the street during nice weather, basic games like hopscotch or "Run Sheep Run." In the summer, when they did not have to go to bed early, they would sit around in the playground and tell spooky stories with their friends. Sometimes they would be able to go to a movie shown at the Duquesne Plaza. In those days they free coupons used to come in a loaf of bread. On the rare occasions when Verona would buy bread at the store instead of baking her own, the older children used to fight over who would use the coupon and would end up taking turns. The cost of admission was only about a nickel, but still practically out of reach for families like my mother's during the Depression.

Anna's favorite form of entertainment was the annual school picnic at Kennywood Park. All the children liked Kennywood—the local amusement park where families, school, lodge and church groups flocked in the spring and summer months to enjoy picnics, rides and games. The park was originally called "Kenny's Grove," after Charles K. Kenny, who purchased the original tract of land, twelve miles from Pittsburgh, and two miles from Homestead, in 1818, for just five pounds, ten shillings, a six pence, and a barrel of whiskey. At that time, people reached "Kenny's Grove" by horse and buggy or via steamboats on the river; it was a haven away from the hard work and drudgery of everyday life, and Charles Kenny let the people use the park free of charge.

At the turn of the century, the concept of the trolley park was being developed around the country. By developing parks that provided games, rides, and shows to entertain people, the Trolley companies hoped to increase ridership on their lines. In Pittsburgh, the Monongahela Street Railway Company wanted to build a trolley park at Kenny's Grove since the Monongahela trolley line trolley went from Oakland, through Squirrel Hill to Homestead, and finally through Kenny's Grove to Duquesne. In 1898, the Monongahela Street Railway Company leased the 141 acres that included Kenny's Grove, from Charles Kenny's grandson, Anthony. Not long after the name "Kennywood" was applied to the park by the well-known bank owner, Andrew Mellon. It started as an open-air casino, and soon a dance pavilion, bandstand, and carousel were built over the years. To keep pace with the appeal of other trolley parks, thrill rides such as rollercoasters were soon added.

Anna remembers buying tickets in school for the annual picnic day at the rate of eight for a dollar. Each child in her family got only a few dollars worth because that was all her parents could afford. Verona would pack a picnic basket lunch—ground up bologna mixed with sweet pickles and mayonnaise, some bananas and some cookies—and sit under one of the shady oak or maple trees that were a trademark of the park while the went on the Ferris Wheel, the Tumblebug, the Whip, and other rides. With the refreshment tickets also purchased in school, the children were able to have a treat of soda pop, or perhaps some popcorn as they left the park to go home at the end of the day. As children they enjoyed the novelty. In later years, the boys would go to work there.

These outings provided some of the fondest memories for Anna, and she did not think about the bad times.

It was around this age of 11 that Anna became aware of the bicultural world in which she was growing up. For mother and her siblings, the mixing of the old and the new was a natural process, where they had the best of both cultures. Typically, the first Slovak children born in America grew up surrounded by the traditions of Slovakia. Their food, music, and holiday celebrations had the stamp of the Old World, but eventually took on American customs.

For example, they celebrated the American holiday of Thanksgiving, complete with turkey and all the trimmings. They also celebrated two Christmases, the first on December 25th and the second on January 7th according to the Byzantine calendar. Because it was more universal, the family would have a big celebration on December 25th which included the secular

60

traditions of a Christmas tree and Santa Claus, but would go to church for January 7th. On the "American" Christmas day the family would spend the day at home. While my mother remembers them always having a Christmas tree, gifts were scarce because her parents could not afford to buy them. The children would have fruits and nuts put in their stockings, and usually got clothes. Mother remembers receiving a baby doll and carriage one year and her brother John a scooter.

For the January 7th Christmas, they would celebrate on the evening before, the traditional supper called the *Vilia*. As she had with her family in Slovakia, Verona spent all day preparing the meal, a meatless supper in keeping with her religious belief that Christmas Eve was a time for fasting. According to custom, the foods prepared for this supper were based on the elements of nature and the fruits of the year's labors.

Before the meal began, Jánoš, as the head of the household, would ask God to bless the food they were about to eat and then the *Vilia* supper would begin. They would consume a sour soup called *kapusnica* made of sauerkraut and mushrooms and *pagach*, a Slovak version of a pizza, filled with sauerkraut or a potato and cheese mixture and baked to a golden brown. Next they would eat *bobalky*, little, baked balls of dough. Depending on which area of Slovakia you came from, *bobalky* were either steamed with milk and coated with poppy seed and/or honey, or browned in butter and a preparation of sauerkraut. Verona followed the sauerkraut recipe. The main course was *pirohi,* (pillows of dough similar to ravioli) filled with cabbage, prunes, dried cottage cheese or potato and cheese and drenched in browned butter, which was sometimes eaten with a serving of fried fish. After the main meal came the dessert which consisted on walnut or poppy seed rolls and all sorts of *kolaci* (cookies). The Christmas Eve celebration culminated as the family, except Jánoš, went to midnight mass. Around the time of Helen's birth, Jánoš had a falling out with the priest and from that day on refused to attend church. The dispute was over money, possibly the priest wanted to charge to baptize the new baby, and Jánoš with his stubborn pride believed this was unacceptable. While he believed in God, he had no use for the organized church

61

or its priests and spoke of how priests earned an easy living without doing any work. Jánoš' bitterness toward the church was so strong that he even prevented John Jr. from making his First Holy Communion as a child. The boy came home one day from catechism class and told his father that the priest beat his hands because he did not make the sign of the cross correctly and Jánoš told him he had no business being in the class anyway. John Jr. took what his father said to heart and did not go back to catechism class, and would not make his Communion until he became an adult. Verona, although deeply hurt by her son's impiety regarding communion, still insisted that he attend church with her and the other children every Sunday, despite her husband's absence. It especially bothered Verona when her husband did not attend church with the family on Holy days, like Christmas or Easter.

Easter was also celebrated twice. For family purposes, Verona recognized the American date for Easter, and that of her religion, which fell two weeks later. For Slovaks, Easter and Lent, the church season leading up to the feast, were taken seriously. Slovaks observed very strict fast and abstinence laws during Lent, and looked forward to Easter, the feast of the Resurrection of Jesus Christ, which to them, was the greatest of all feasts because it combined the Christian celebration of Christ with the old Slovak pagan custom of marking the renewal of the earth in the Spring. The children remember their mother spending hours in the kitchen preparing special foods they ate only once a year.

Mother remembered spending many hours in church in the days leading up to Easter. On Holy Thursday, Verona and the children would go to church to commemorate the Lord's Supper; for Catholics it was the day when the Holy Eucharist was instituted by Jesus' breaking bread with his apostles. On Good Friday, they attended services in the afternoon, and the mood for the entire day was a somber one. Verona did the minimum of work on that day, and the children were not listen to the radio during the hours leading up to the service, as they were supposed to pray and remember the Lord's death. On Saturday, preparations for the Slovak Easter feast began. Verona rose early and began making *paska* or Easter bread, a special sweet yeast bread baked as a round loaf with a golden crust and a yellow center made from eggs, butter, and white raisins. *Paska* was made to commemorate the fact that Jesus is the living bread from heaven in the Eucharist. She also prepared a custard-type round cheese called *hrudka*, or *syrek*, made from eggs and milk simmered slowly until it separated into curds and whey. She would spoon the curds into a cheesecloth and shape it into a ball. The corners of the cloth were then tied together and she would hang the ball in the basement over the laundry tub until it became firm. The cheese, with its bland but sweet taste, symbolized the moderation that Christians should have in all things. The children colored and decorated eggs, in Slovak called *pisanky*. Verona also prepared *chren* (beets mixed with horseradish—as a reminder of the bitter herbs which the Israelites had during their Passover supper, and also of the bitter drink the Lord was given while he hung on the cross), and a special sausage known as *klobassy* indicative of God's favor and generosity. She also baked a ham to celebrate the freedom of the New Law, which came into effect with the resurrection of Jesus. Slovaks ate ham instead of lamb, which is the traditional Passover meat because lamb was not readily available to them in the old country and they carried the custom to the New World.

On Holy Saturday, Verona would pack a large wicker basket filled with these foods, cover it with a special crocheted cloth (which, to this day, is still in the family), and take it to our church to be blessed by the priest. After the blessing, the foods were ready to eat on Easter Sunday, after church. The family gathered to celebrate in the joy of the risen Lord, exchanging with one another the traditional greeting of "Christos Voskres" (Christ is Risen!).

The children fondly remembered the holiday times, especially because of the emphasis on family and the observance of special customs. As my mother recalled, "They always tried to make our holidays nice, Christmas, Thanksgiving, and it was just the family and we were close."

Jánoš and Verona tried to teach their children Slovak ways, but being in the mainstream (especially attending the public school as opposed to the established Slovak parish or parochial schools), the children saw the New World all around them—a world that was theirs to discover. Born American, they hoped to grow up American—just like those children with whom they went to school. Even before their children started the process in earnest, Verona and János, like other Slovak immigrants, had already taken some steps toward assimilation. One of the most notable forms of assimilation came with the way they dressed. Back in Slovakia, people typically wore two types of clothing. There were work garments made of white linen of seasonal weight, and then the more elaborately embroidered folk dress worn by men and women for holidays and special occasions. In America they adopted fashions of the time. János wore jeans or overalls when working in the mill and a black suit for formal occasions. Verona wore simple cotton dresses during the week and perhaps a white dress on Sunday or a black dress for funerals, but her traditional costumes were only brought out occasionally for weddings or Slovak feast days.

As for their diets, Slovak immigrants changed them only slightly upon arrival and János insisted on eating the foods he ate back in Slovakia—a simple diet of potatoes, cheeses, milk, sauerkraut, and thick vegetable soups with vinegar or sour cream. For Slovaks, it was not uncommon for their diet to remain unchanged for many years. Once the second generation tired of preparing traditional recipes changes in diet began to take place. The children embraced American foods, such as macaroni and cheese, hamburgers, ice cream, candy and soda pop.

Entertainment and sports also played roles in the assimilation process. When attending the fraternal lodge or saloon or special occasions like weddings, János enjoyed the traditional folk music played by gypsy bands to which they danced the waltzes, *czardas* and polkas, but in everyday life, entertainment in America meant popular tunes played on radios and phonographs.

Even as first generation immigrants, János and Verona did not seem to have a terribly difficult time assimilating into American lifestyle. Perhaps it is because they came to America at a later date than many first generation immigrants. Whereas the big waves of Slovak immigration came during the 1880s and 1890s and before WWI, when it seemed that Slovaks poured into North America. Jánoš and Verona came in the 1920s and in 1924, Slovak immigration to the United States virtually halted because of the immigration quota system that set limits on the number of people from each country who could enter the United States each year which discriminated against the Slovaks and other southern and eastern Europeans in favor of northern and western Europeans. Those earlier immigrants (arriving after 1870 or so) created communities that reflected Old World communities—people who practiced the same religion, spoke the same dialect, enjoyed same food and music and felt a kinship that helped them survive harsh living and working conditions and preserve their native culture and maintain a distinct Slovak identity in North America. The early immigrants established churches, schools, fraternal benefit societies and Slovak organizations that made life easier for them than it had been for those who came before and certainly made life and adjustment less traumatic for those who came after.

During this time, Anna remembers her father taking the train to Pittsburgh to file some papers, which would eventually lead to him becoming an American citizen. One day he would appear in court and be expected to answer many questions in front of a man called a judge. Although at this age she did not fully understand the significance of this process or how it was a step towards assimilation, a voluntary separation from his homeland and a symbolic breaking away from his Slovak culture, she knew it meant something to her father and that he wanted to become an "American." She did not know when exactly the day would come, but sensed that when it did, it would truly be a happy occasion.

CHAPTER EIGHT
DISCIPLINE

My mother remembered kneeling behind the black coal stove in the basement of the house on Crawford Avenue. Each strike of the leather strap—first across her shoulders, then over her back and legs—stung more than the last one. Large red welts appeared on her body, but the physical pain was nothing compared to her fear and embarrassment. She thought he would never stop. When he finally did, she sobbed and lifted herself from the floor. In spite of the beating, she did not hate her father; she vowed not to do anything wrong again and wanted to please him.

Anna was only 12 years old when she received the beating from her father. It was the most significant event she remembered from her childhood years and one that remained imprinted in her memory. Although it was the first and last time he would hit her with such severity, the beating shaped the way she viewed him from then on. She had not thought he would miss the $12 she secretly removed from the purse in the kitchen cabinet to treat one of her junior high school friends to ice cream at Vezdel's corner store. After all, it was her turn to buy. Her friend, who always seemed to have money, usually bought candy, pop, and ice cream for both of them. Anna did not have the money, but she knew her father did. As treasurer of a local Slovak fraternal lodge, he had cash stored away in a dresser drawer. With her father's money, she too could feel like a big shot.

The year was 1937, hard times, especially hard for a laborer trying to provide for a wife and five children, with another baby on the way. After seven years of pleading with the U.S. Steel employment office in Pittsburgh for work and two years on WPA and Welfare, Anna's father had just obtained a steady job in the cindering plant at the Duquesne mill.

My mother recalled that under such meager living conditions, the missing $12 seemed more like $12,000 to her father. He repeatedly yelled, "Who took my money?" until she confessed. Then he beat her and threatened to send her to

66

Morganza, a home for bad children. Her mother, Verona, pleaded with him to stop, afraid that he was going to kill his daughter. Anna promised to pay back him back as soon as she was old enough to find a job, and she did, once she was in high school and found a job at the local five and dime store in the Duquesne Plaza. When Anna received her first pay she went, with tears welling in her eyes, to her father to apologize and give him the money, which János refused to take until she pleaded he do so, saying, "I know it has been awhile, but I promised to pay you back."

Anna's beating was just one example of the kind of strict discipline she and her six siblings experienced at the hands of their father, who insisted on following old European ways when rearing his children. One of the greatest problems faced by Slavic immigrants in the transition from the old country to the new was that of family life. In Slovakia, households were governed by the patriarchal system where the word of the parents and, most especially the father, was law. The home was a gathering place for the entire family and their friends. The children respected the position of their father and were trained to obey, and "to be good soldiers, not good citizens". If the child revolted, the entire neighborhood turned against him. The husband exerted his right to choose the home, to discipline his wife and children, to claim their services, appropriate their earnings, and manage all the affairs of the household. But in America, freedom made the conditions entirely different, and some Slovak fathers discovered that they were unable to maintain the same authority as in Europe, but not János. His favorite saying was, "I'm the boss," and there was no arguing with him. He had a temper that was easily provoked. Once, in junior high school, Anna took a chance on a raffle and won a box of Coty's face powder, but because she was forbidden to wear make-up, her father threw the container into the coal stove. János also demanded that his children show respect for their mother, and if any of them dared not, her, especially if they referred to their mother as "she" or "her," he would raise his voice to them, saying, "Who is she? You don't say she, that's your mother."

My mother recalled her father being especially strict with her. When out with her friends, she had to be in by 9:00 and even when she became a senior in high school she was not allowed to date. He did not want her to become interested in boys and get distracted from her studies. He also feared that she might become sexually involved and get pregnant. Instead, Jánoš wanted her to finish school and graduate, not to improve her chances for marriage as was the goal typically found among immigrant parents, but because he wanted her to be able to find a job to support herself if she needed to. Anna believed that her father was harder on her because she was the oldest. He and Verona also expected her to look after her younger siblings, and if they got into trouble, so did she. Anna obeyed her father, perhaps more out of fear than anything else.

Most times when Jánoš disciplined his children, Verona would just stand by defenseless, aware that even if she dared to say something, her words would not stop him. My mother does not recall Verona hitting her. Whenever her husband was at work, Verona would often correct the children verbally if they did something wrong, and if they did not stop, then would threaten to tell their father when he came home and he would be the disciplinarian.

Out of all the children, only John Jr. remembered being beaten by Verona. He recalled how one particular time he spoke disrespectfully to an elderly woman while he was out with Verona. Verona was so angry with her son that when they returned home she beat him with a stick. She would also punish him for not coming home on time, not doing his chores or sneaking out of the house. As an adult, he reflected back on those times noting that he thought she was tougher on him perhaps because he gave her more of a problem than any of the other children, and while he knew he had a place in her heart as the eldest son, he also knew she relied on him and Anna to help keep the younger children in line.

The one matter Jánoš enforced with all of his children was education. He was always around to sign their report cards; he wanted them to receive good grades, and if the marks were not up to standard, he would punish first and ask questions later.

For example, one time Anna brought home a report card with a D grade that was really supposed to be an "A," and her father punished her without letting her explain why the grade was so low. He also refused to sign the report card. The next day Anna went to the teacher with her unsigned report card and the teacher discovered she had given Anna the wrong grade and corrected it. Anna showed her father the corrected grade and he was satisfied.

Jánoš pushed the issue of his children's education because he wanted them to make something of themselves. Only 20 percent of the children of early immigrants graduated from high school; they had to work at a young age because their families were so poor. For many first generation Slavs, their own education did not go beyond simple reading, writing and arithmetic and they did not see a high school diploma as necessary for sons who would spend their lives working in a mine or a mill, or daughters who would become housewives. Jánoš thought the opposite and wanted all of his children to finish high school. He especially did not want his sons to follow in his footsteps by going to work in the mills or mines and wanted them to have more choices in life.

As my mother remembered, my grandfather's dominance over the family—in just about every matter—prevailed throughout her teenage years and her fear of him remained even after she became an adult.

CHAPTER NINE
"DR. JEKYLL" AND "MR. HYDE"

By 1938, times were getting better for the family. Now that Jánoš had secured a steady job in the mill, the family could not only afford to pay their rent, but to buy luxuries, such as a radio, which enabled them to listen to Pittsburgh Pirate baseball games, as well as such popular programs as "Inner Sanctum" and the "Lone Ranger" and a Maytag washer so that Verona would no longer have to boil her clothes and scrub them by hand. With the birth of their third daughter, Geraldine, in May of that year, there were now six children and Verona had extra diapers to wash in addition to all of her children's clothes and her husband's soiled work pants and shirts, so having the washer made Verona's work life a degree easier.

In having a steady job, Jánoš gained back his confidence and self-respect. He prided himself in being a "good worker." The children recalled how the first time he came home with a full two weeks' pay, Jánoš slapped a $100 bill down on the kitchen table to show his wife and children he was the bread winner of the family. Jánoš' strong work ethic was passed down to his children. Even with his steady job, the older children had to work at a young age to earn their own spending money. Anna was 12 years old when she began scrubbing floors, obtaining jobs through word of mouth at church or in the neighborhood. For each job, she would earn about a dollar and would save her money until she had enough to have her hair permed or buy something she wanted. Her brothers, John and Joe were just 11 or 12 when they began working Saturdays cleaning chickens at a nearby poultry store. Several years later, when the boys turned fourteen they went to work at Kennywood amusement park as many teenage boys were inclined to do. It was part of a Slovak's character to work hard, and Jánoš taught his children to take pride in their work, whether household chores such as doing the dishes or shoveling coal, or the jobs they performed to earn a wage.

A year after first getting a job in the mill, Jánoš transferred from the cindering plant to work in the ore yard. There he worked eight hours a day, whether in 90-degree heat when his clothes stuck like glue against his sweat-covered body or in the biting cold of winter when he wore extra thick long underwear beneath his work pants and shirt. Ore, along with coke and limestone, were the three essential components used to produce steel. The iron ore came from the regions surrounding Lake Superior and was carried across the Great Lakes in the company's own vessels and transported by cars on the Bessemer and Lake Erie Railroad to the Duquesne Works. Coke and limestone dug from the hills of Pennsylvania came via the Pittsburgh, Virginia and Charleston Railroad. Upon reaching the stockyard, which stretched along the length of the furnace plant, the three materials had to be separated into bins along furnace. There were two series of bins, one set of ore bins, and then the coke and limestone bins.

Jánoš rode a railroad car called the "Hopper," which had a platform on top where he stood to work the hand brake to slow down the car at the ore dumper. The ore was then transferred to the "Larry" car, which another man drove to the ore trestle that led from the mill. Sometimes his job was to stand on the trestle to open the doors of the "Larry" car. The ore was emptied from the "Larry" car onto the trestle, where a crane then lifted the ore into different stockpiles in pits—one for African ore, one for Brazilian ore, and so on. Anna remembers her father being covered with red dust when he came home after his shift ended.

As dirty as the job in ore yard was, it provided Jánoš with a steady enough income that he soon moved his family out of the house at 129 Crawford Avenue into a wooden home, with a flat roof, which they rented on Cochran Avenue, a few blocks away from the mill. At one time the houses were owned by U.S. Steel and rented out to workers, but at the time Jánoš rented the houses had been turned over to a private owner. The house was part of a two family building with Jánoš' family living on one side and the Kulic family living on the other. The houses were set up in a courtyard area, with other families living in similar houses only across the yard. There were families from a variety of ethnic

71

backgrounds: Spanish, Russian, Hungarian, African-American, and quite a few struggling Slovak families whose men, like Jánoš, worked in the mill. The interior of the house consisted of a living room and kitchen downstairs and two bedrooms upstairs. The cellar was nothing more than a dirt floor, and Anna was afraid to go down there because of its dark and dreary atmosphere. While the family had the convenience of running water, the house lacked an indoor toilet and the family was forced to use an outhouse lined up next to those belonging to the other families in the courtyard. All the people living there were struggling Slovak families whose men worked in the mill.

Although the family lived in four rooms instead of two, living space was still cramped because Verona took in steelworkers as boarders to help pay the rent, which at the time was quite cheap. Because of the boarders, Verona was able to save a little money each month with the hope that she and Jánoš could buy their own place someday.

The boarders shared one of the upstairs bedrooms, which left six children to sleep in the other. Verona and Jánoš slept downstairs on the sleeper-sofa. Providing for the boarders placed heavy demands on Verona. There were meals to cook, clothes to wash, lunch buckets to prepare. The boarders were always served their meals first, then the family. Unlike her husband who occasionally had a day off from his labor in the mill, she had little reprieve from her tasks.

Jánoš soon found his own reprieve from work at one of the nearby drinking establishments. The house on Cochran was closer not only to the mill but also to the neighborhood bar, Legin's Café. Legin's was her husband's usual stop for a "shot and a beer" after his daylight shift in the mill ended. For men like Jánoš, a stop at the local bar after work was quite common. The monotony of many types of work and the competitive drive of the entire industrial system, with its emphasis on materialism often resulted in frustrations. Thus saloons and taverns were an accepted part of working class culture. As community establishments, neighborhood taverns were more than just places for men to drink, they served as a venue where they could visit with one another to

72

share their complaints about company policy, discuss problems or politics, and play cards or other games to help them forget the drudgery of their everyday lives. In the early days, a tavern also functioned as a center of information and services, serving as a place where the immigrant could find temporary lodging, find an interpreter or translator, ask someone to notarize papers, perform banking transactions such as obtaining credit, depositing savings, or purchasing a money order to send home. Often taverns served as a hiring hall where bosses from the mines or mills could find available labor. Such business transactions were easily and conveniently done in saloons or taverns because they opened early and closed late. Alcoholic drinking in neighborhood taverns played a secondary role. Working people rarely met in each others' homes for social activities as the middle class did. Friends and acquaintances formed a type of social society with a drink serving as the only price of admission. Thus, drink became inseparable from social activity, relaxation and pleasure.

For Jánoš , the bar served as a place where he found a sense of belonging; a place in the community, where he sought friendship during his leisure time. Jánoš usually never left the bar until he was drunk.

Eventually the occasional stops became more frequent. Jánoš would routinely stop at Legin's whenever he worked the 7 to 3 shift or the 3 to 11 shift. If Jánoš worked night-turn (11 to 7) he went straight home to sleep, but when he had a day off, he would spend several hours and sometimes the entire day at the bar.

Verona began to anticipate when her husband would be drunk. In the nice weather she would sit on the porch and wait for him to come home. As soon as her husband came into sight, Verona threw her hands up, sighed a deep sigh, and went into the house. If he was close enough to view her actions, his face became flushed with anger and his head filled with false notions of his wife's imagined infidelity, or some other fault on her part. Once home he began to make demands. If his supper was not on the table—even if it was 2:00 a.m.—he would yell obscenities at his wife in Slovak. Often he hit her. On those occasions when the dish she prepared was not to his liking, he would hurl his plate across the table.

My mother recalled that her father did not begin to drink heavily until after the move to Cochran Avenue. Prior to that he drank only on special occasions, such as weddings and funerals but rarely drank at home. The whiskey he kept in the cabinet was for relatives or friends who visited on Sunday, when sometimes he would drink a shot or two with the visitor. All that changed with the move.

To my mother, her father became a "Dr. Jekyll-Mr. Hyde." While sober, he was a man who never missed a day on the job and worked hard to provide food, clothing and a home for his family. He would stay up late to help her with a difficult math assignment; he played card games such as "Steal the Pile" and "500 Rummy," built puzzles with her and her siblings, and enjoyed telling a good joke. He cared for their well-being. Mother remembered that he had a beautiful face and, when he smiled, how his blue eyes would sparkle. But when he was drank he was full of rage. My mother recalled that liquor transformed his naturally fickle temper into a violent rage that was difficult to stop. Mother, who feared and hated these tirades, usually stood and watched as he took out his frustration on her mother. Once he hit her on the ear. Another time he hit her for being ill and not getting out of bed to cook for him. On more than one occasion when he was out of control, Verona would gather her six children and walk to her sister's home in the Polish Hill section of Duquesne while her husband slept off his drunken state. He hit his children only to punish them or when they stepped in to prevent him from hitting their mother.

Paydays were the worst. Twice a month the long-awaited day arrived. A time both welcomed and feared by my grandmother. It meant she could pay the rent, settle her accounts with the butcher and grocer, and hopefully have some money left over to put away in the little tin box. But payday also meant trouble. If her husband did not come home within a few hours of quitting time, Verona knew he would not stop drinking until all the money was gone, so she would send one of the boys to bring him home or to collect what was left of his paycheck. My mother also

74

feared paydays. This was when her father drank the most and was the most violent.

As the children grew older they had to intercede for their mother more frequently. The three sons would step in and could usually control him, although he would not think twice about attacking anyone who stood in his way including his sons. One time, when John Jr. was already in high school, Jánoš almost tore the shirt off of John's back. Jánoš had chased after John and was going to throw him down the cellar steps, but John was able to break away, leaving his torn shirt behind. John went outside with his mother and sat on porch until Jánoš cooled off.

Another time, he came home from Legin's in a foul mood and began chasing Verona and John Jr. with a chair. Jánoš was so out of control that even three teenage boys could not hold him back, and in order to get him to calm down they called the police, who took him away to jail for the night.

It is anyone's guess as to what provoked Jánoš that time, or any of the others, but as his children remember, these sprees were often initiated by something that happened at the bar. Perhaps he lost a card game (he was an excellent card player and hated to lose) or possibly he had words with a fellow patron who made him angry. He may have looked around the bar and saw people he thought were not as smart as him yet they had better jobs. But instead of taking it out on the source, he brought whatever anxieties or troubles caused by these encounters home with him, and then after he came home, Verona provoked him into an argument, as she was apt to do on more than one occasion. She knew that some of the men at the bar aggravated him, so would suggest that if he wanted a drink he had his liquor at home and then he would not run into the guys he didn't like or get along with. Also, money was tight so she would begrudge him his visits to the bar, "You work so hard, you are just going to the bar and drinking away whatever you earn." This would be enough to set him off. He thought he deserved to stop for a drink after all of his hard work. As the children remembered, he wanted to be recognized for the job that he did and if he couldn't earn it among his fellow workers, he would get it at home. He wanted to attract his family's attention. If he thought he was being avoided or ignored, he would break open with these sprees. As long as there was someone there to give him attention, to squeal or scream, he would keep up the tirade, but if he had a chance to sit there alone and think then there would be no problem. They knew his job in the mill contributed to his feelings of frustration, perhaps because Jánoš felt he was employed way below his qualifications. He was a bright man, maybe not in the way of a formal education, but certainly in real life issues. Jánoš was also a good speaker, a good organizer and leader and skilled with his hands. But he really did not have a choice where his occupation was concerned. He was reaching out for something else, but since he was limited by his circumstances really could not achieve it. The alcohol was a release for him, it was a way to deal with the stress and kill his pain.

As Jánoš' outbursts became more frequent, so did the children's desire to protect their mother. She was the foundation, the one who held the family together. They loved her and did not want any harm to come to her, especially at the hands of their father. She was the one who was at home with them all day. She cooked their meals, washed and mended their clothes, kept the house immaculately clean despite the smoke and dust from the mill which made dirt a constant nuisance. She attended to their emotional and spiritual needs and saw to it that they had a moral and religious upbringing, wanting them to be good and not hear a bad word spoken about any of them. She managed the family's finances so that they would have food on the table, stretching each dollar but still able to make meals that tasted good. The children felt sorry for their mother—a woman whose life seemed to be all work, and dreaded seeing their father come home and scream at her, call her names, and hit her.

It was not uncommon for Slovak men to get drunk during life's toughest moments, and they often used this as an excuse for beating their wives. The wives took it because they knew their husbands were miserable. Husbands would shout at their wives and children. As Lillian Dawson, a social worker from the Pittsburgh area during the 1930s wrote, "If you grew up in coal and steel communities as I did, you saw the toll these industries took on the men. But the final price? it was paid by their women."

John Jr. remembered that there did not seem to be any household on the block where a drunken father wasn't yelling at the mother or children and in some homes incidents occurred that were physically worse, with blood and people being chased out with knives.

While Jánoš never resorted to using knives or other weapons, nevertheless, his violent outbursts were serious enough to evoke painful recollections in my mother and her siblings even when they became adults. These incidents caused them to fear their father sometimes the fear even turned to hatred on occasion. Helen, who was just a very young girl at the time, remembers living in constant fear of her father and hating him for what he was doing to himself and his family. She vowed she would never marry a man who drank and would come home and beat her as she watched her father do to her mother. Out of all the children, however, my mother seemed to be affected the most by her father's drinking and violent behavior. His drinking had such a severe impact on my mother, that when she became an adult she did not like to participate in social events where anyone was drinking heavily, and only on rare occasions would she drink alcohol herself. Mother despised bars and the fear of her drunken father's wrath stayed with her always, like an open sore that never seemed to heal.

CHAPTER TEN
BREAKING AWAY

In 1942 the family moved to another house, this time located at Hickory Alley. It was a frame, two-family duplex. The Zosoms, who lived on one side, were already settled when Jánoš moved his family in to the other half. The house had four rooms—two rooms downstairs and two upstairs bedrooms, one of which the boarders moved into. While the house lacked a full, finished bathroom, there was a toilet in the basement so the family no longer had to use an outhouse. The move was prompted by Verona's desire for a cleaner living environment. She despised the cockroaches and other bugs which infested the flat, wooden house on Cochran Street. Jánoš began to ask around work and the bar and found out that a French man named Moreau owned some houses down at the very bottom of Crawford not far from their current place and he went to inquire about renting one of them. Jánoš' job in the ore yard provided steady work so they could afford to move.

By this time Jánoš and Verona had both obtained American citizenship. Jánoš had taken the oath of allegiance in January of 1939 and had little difficulty when the judge asked him questions about America, such as "Who was the first President?" or asked to recite the National Anthem or Pledge of Allegiance. He wanted to become a citizen and to permanently reside in the United States, as he had nothing to return to in Czechoslovakia since his mother had died and he was not particularly close with his other siblings or relatives who remained there. He also had a family of his own now to worry about and wanted a better life for his children. It was a big step for my grandfather to renounce his homeland after being a loyal soldier and proud of his heritage, but I suppose like many immigrants the idea of "the land of the free" was quite appealing. My mother recalled how being able to vote in elections was important to him and he lectured her and her siblings often about exercising this privilege.

In February of 1941, two years after Jánoš, Verona acquired her U.S. citizenship. She was not as confident as Jánoš. When Verona received her letter to appear in court in downtown Pittsburgh, she had her children help her practice the answers to the questions. Her neighbor on Crawford Street, and close friend, Mrs. Irene Carroll and her brother-in-law, John Kolcun, served as her witnesses as she appeared in front of the judge.

The acquisition of American citizenship surely had to be a moment of mixed emotions for my grandmother. The event must have seemed a climax to that long journey she had made almost 20 years earlier. On paper she was American, now one step further removed from her heritage. Perhaps she did not realize it at the time, but it was a sort of a symbolic breaking away from tradition and the beginning of a culture slipping away, a culture her children and grandchildren would have to struggle to hold on to as they would no longer be called Slovak but would have a hyphenated heritage as Slovak-Americans.

As her mother was becoming a U.S. citizen, Anna was at the age where she started to gain her own independence. They were still living at Hickory Alley when Anna graduated from high school in June of 1943. Her parents did not have enough money to send her to college; however, she was able to follow a secretarial/business curriculum in high school and did well enough to be hired as a secretary for the Westinghouse Corporation soon after she graduated. The office was located in East Pittsburgh, and Anna took a streetcar to and from work each day. Part of her salary went to her parents. The opportunity of acquiring a secretarial job was just one of the advantages Anna had over her mother, who as a young woman could only find work as a domestic. Thus, employment was yet another factor which served to separate the generations.

Two weeks after Anna graduated from high school, Verona gave birth to her seventh and final child—a baby girl whom they named Margaret Alice but called Margie.

Approximately a year after Margie's birth, the family moved, for the last time, to a seven-room, two-story frame house on Hill Street. They paid approximately $4,000 for the house, with a $2,000 down payment and paid off the balance of the mortgage within a very short time. The purchase was made possible primarily by Verona's thriftiness over the years. Jánoš had worked overtime and with the cheap rent, she was able to pinch her pennies. She was not extravagant in anything. For example she rarely bought clothes for her children, rather they wore hand-me-downs and the family ate the cheapest food she could make. The older children also helped out by contributing a portion of their earnings to the savings. If Verona had not been able to secretly stash away a little here and there, they never would have had anything because Jánoš surely would have spent the extra funds on alcohol.

One of Jánoš' friends used his truck to move the family's things. Besides their clothes, they had few possessions—the coal stove, a studio couch, table and chairs, two beds, the baby's crib, radio and Verona's sewing machine and washer. The one thing that did stand out in my mother's mind was how proud Verona and Jánoš were to finally own their own home. It provided a sense of security and place, considerations that were important to Slovaks, because they remembered how, as peasants, they had to work off of someone else's land. Together, they finally achieved a status that was higher than they had ever known since they came to America, which reflected years of struggling and hard work. Mother and her siblings thought they were in heaven. They had running water, a refrigerator, and finally, a full indoor bathroom complete with toilet, sink and bathtub, which meant no more baths in the wooden tub. They were equally as happy that the two boarders did not come with them. Since Jánoš was bringing in a steady paycheck they no longer depended on the extra money.

By the time Jánoš and Verona were settling into this new home they watched their older children, Anna, John Jr. and Joe, become increasingly self-sufficient, while they still had four younger children to raise.

In 1944, John Jr. graduated high school, and after six months of working in the mill, he decided to join the Navy. Since he was only 17, he had to have his father sign papers granting him permission. Jánoš was reluctant, but since WWII was already in

80

full force, it was possible that his son would be drafted anyway, so he agreed. Perhaps as other young immigrant men, John saw the military as a way to better himself and to escape having to work in the mill. Anna and Joe went down to the train station to see their brother off. John Jr. was the first of the siblings to leave home and break away from Jánoš' rule and Verona's loving care. It was the last time John, Anna and Joe would be that close as brothers and sister. From then on things would be different—the familial bonds would be stretched and would never be the same or as strong as before he left.

Verona found it difficult to watch her eldest son leave, but she did not try to stop him. In her heart she knew he had to go and find his own way, as she had done herself when she left her mother all those years ago. With John, Jr. gone the responsibility of protecting Verona against their father's violent outbursts now fell to Joe and Mike.

In fact, not much changed on the home front or between Jánoš and Verona. Verona had hoped that her husband's stops at the bar would become less frequent, but this did not happen. She thought that perhaps the new baby might entice him to spend more time at home and that with the move, he would not be so close to Legin's and this would prevent his drunken sprees. But Jánoš found another bar, the Union Grill, located at the corner of Crawford Avenue and Fifth Street, just one block away from their home on Hill Street. The Union Grill, was another popular hangout for the Duquesne millworkers, and in particular for those of Slovak descent. On average the bar held 30 men or more after the daylight shift. During the summer months, the main door to the bar was open and the loud jumbled sound of male voices filtered through the screen and could be heard outside.

Jánoš was a faithful customer. He would enter through the front door, and head directly to the bar to order his quart of whiskey and his glass of beer, then sit down at his usual table, with his buddies, Bucky (the mushroom man) and the two Mikes. The four men always sat at the first table closest to the front door. Often they played cards. Sometimes Euchre and 500 Rummy, but mostly Pinochle. Other times the guys just sat and talked, usually

81

about politics, work, or the date of the next outing to pick mushrooms. Whether or not he went to the bar to socialize or because he wanted a drink was difficult to pinpoint and his children tended not to believe that their father was a true "alcoholic." My mother remembered that his drinking spells occurred mostly around the times he got paid. He rarely drank at home (he had an occasional beer when he played cards with visitors or Solitaire on his day off) and did not drink first thing in the morning. He never missed a day's work on account of his drinking. But it was no secret that the men in his family liked to drink. His brothers, Jacob and Joseph, and Simeon (Sam) were also heavy drinkers.

Instead of dealing with him, the children who still lived at home learned to plan their schedules around his shifts in the mill in order to prevent outbursts if they wanted to go out, or not feel embarrassed by his behavior if they had friends or dates over to the house. Heaven help them if he came home drunk and something was out of place, or he found a light bulb burned out, or discovered that one of the girls had run too much water for her bath.

While the fear of their father's violent outbursts provided a good reason for Anna and her siblings to spend as little time as possible in the home, it may have been a convenient excuse for them to start the process of breaking away—of separating themselves from the old ways associated with home life and moving into an American lifestyle more suited for their generation. In this respect they were no different than the children of other Slavic immigrants. Small crowded homes did not allow for young people to entertain their friends. They preferred to go to the movies or visit the local parks, or invented other excuses to get away from home. In further rebellion some children refused to attend the dances and club meetings of the national organizations with their parents. Many broken homes resulted from the rebellion of the second generation. In my mother's case, life at home was tumultuous but not broken. The family and home were kept together by Verona.

82

CHAPTER ELEVEN
ONE GENERATION REMOVED

The Second World War ended in 1945, sending home many of the youth who had been drafted to serve their country. John Anthony Alzo (or Johnny as his family and friends called him) was among them. He was discharged fom the Navy on St. Patrick's Day 1946 after serving for two years in the Pacific, on tanker ships that transported troops and gasoline. The life of a seaman did not appeal to Johnny and he was anxious to return home to Duquesne and get a job. For many young men Johnny's age, getting a job meant going to work in the mill. It was possible that Johnny might be able to get back his old job of oiling turbine engines in the blowing room of the blast furnace department, where he had worked for two months after his high school graduation prior to being drafted.

When Johnny came back to Duquesne, he went to live with his parents, John and Elizabeth Alzo, who had emigrated from Slovakia through Ellis Island before the First World War. Johnny was their youngest of four children and the only boy among three sisters—Anna, Elizabeth and Helen. A fifth child, Agnes had died at birth.

John Alzo Sr., or Jánoš Alsio (pronounced "awl-zho"), as he was known in Europe), had immigrated to the United States in 1910. He was 16 when he left his home and family in Kucin, Slovakia, to escape induction into the military, and went to join his brother-in-law in McKees Rocks, PA. John was a soft-spoken and religious man with a very pleasant personality. He stood a lanky 5'10, had blond hair and blue eyes, and a distinguishable dimple in his chin. He liked to work with his hands and was good at fixing machines, skills that eventually landed him a job as a millwright at US Steel in Duquesne.

Elisabeth Fencak was also from Slovakia. She was 16 when she left the village of Posa and came to America, in 1914, also through Ellis Island. Upon arrival, Elizabeth went to live with her sister and brother-in-law Anna and George Bavolar, in

83

Duquesne. Elisabeth often visited her other sister, Mary Ceyba, who lived nearby. She met John, who was a boarder there and the two married in January 1915 in St. Peter & Paul Greek Catholic Church, in Duquesne, but later joined the Roman Catholic Church, Holy Trinity. Elisabeth and John became United States citizens in 1928. Young Johnny grew up in the house on Hill Street and went to the Holy Trinity Roman Catholic School through the eighth grade.

When Johnny arrived home from the Navy, he discovered how the dynamics of his family life had changed while he was away. While his eldest sister, Ann, had already left home at age 13 to attend school at a convent in Texas (taking the name Sister M. Camilla). His other sisters, Helen and Betty, were both married. Helen had married Steve Broskovich, and lived in the neighboring town of Swissvale. Elizabeth (Betty) was married to John Berta, and had a two-year-old son, John Jr. (Jackie), but still lived with her parents in the house on Hill Street. Johnny often went along when Betty took her son to the park or zoo. During one of these outings, Betty introduced her brother to her friend Anna Figlar, whom she had invited along, and whose family had moved in next door while Johnny was in the Navy. Anna was an attractive girl with dark hair, green eyes, and a slim figure. The two would each go along with Betty and her family on outings to Kennywood or shopping in East Liberty and soon discovered they had many things in common. They were around the same age with Johnny two months older than Anna and were from Slovak backgrounds. Although they both graduated from Duquesne High School in the same year, they did not know one another well. Johnny was popular; he stood 5'11, with blue eyes and wavy blonde hair—a star forward on the Duquesne High School varsity basketball team. In his junior and senior years, Johnny was in the starting line-up and was one of the high scorers, and had his picture in the local newspaper many times. Anna was not interested in sports and generally concentrated on her studies. She shied away from boys because her father did not permit her to date.

It was not long after these joint outings that Johnny asked Anna out for a date to the movies. Anna had been casually dating different fellows, including Betty's brother-in-law, Mike, but was not involved in a steady relationship. Johnny was much like his own father—soft-spoken, with a friendly personality and sense of humor, and he enjoyed sports and movies.

Not long after Johnny and Anna began to date steadily. Since Johnny did not own a car, they generally went to local venues, places such as Kennywood, which were within walking distance. Sometimes they would take the streetcar to Oakland to watch hockey or the Roller Derby at the Duquesne Gardens.

Johnny had obtained a steady job with Union Railroad in Duquesne, and did an apprenticeship as a carpenter, earning 92 cents an hour. Unlike his father, he turned down the opportunity to go back to the steel mill, because he wanted to work a daylight shift so that he could play basketball at night for teams such as the Duquesne Serbs or CIO.

Within three months Anna and Johnny became engaged. He was planning to give her a ring for her birthday, but surprised her with it a bit earlier, proposing to her on her parents' back porch. Anna went to sleep that night without telling anyone about the engagement. Only Johnny's sister, Betty, knew because she helped him pick out the ring. While Anna was asleep that night, her sisters spotted the platinum ring on her finger and by the next afternoon, everyone in Anna's family knew about her engagement.

Anna's parents were happy about her engagement. After all, Johnny was a Catholic, although a Roman Catholic. Because of this denominational difference, the couple had to obtain permission to marry in Anna's church. Johnny belonged to Holy Trinity; his priest had to approve. Anna was afraid that the priest might not approve the marriage because the he was old-fashioned in his beliefs and practices, and at one time, the Roman Catholic Church would not recognize a marriage to a Greek Catholic. But the approval was granted, with the understanding that after that day, Anna would follow her husband to the Roman Catholic Church.

More importantly, Johnny was of Slovak descent. It was a pattern for second generation Slovaks to marry fellow Slovaks; the only exceptions were those sons or daughters of prosperous

Slovaks who married outside their ethnic group, typically selecting Irish partners whom they married for status because the Irish represented the establishment.

Intermarriage with other ethnic groups provided another common way of assimilating, but for years Slovaks kept to themselves. While the first generation almost never married non-Slovaks, one-third of the second generation married non-Slovaks, but stayed close to their heritage and usually married members of culturally similar ethnic groups: Czechs, Poles, Hungarians, Ukrainians. Anna was the only one of her siblings to marry another Slovak. In subsequent years, her brothers and sisters would break the tradition of Slovak-Slovak unions, and would select partners from Irish, Italian, German, Polish and Russian, backgrounds. Assimilation through intermarriage only became acceptable with later generations (fewer than half of the immigrants' grandchildren and great-grandchildren married other Slovaks and those that married non-Slovaks began to marry a greater proportion of people of northern and western European heritage.

Four months later, on October 14, 1947, Anna Figlar became the bride of John Alzo, Jr. in St. Peter & Paul Greek Catholic Church. It was a balmy Tuesday—an unusual day for a wedding by today's standards—but back then it was not uncommon for couples to marry during the week. The wedding was a much-anticipated event, especially for Anna's family, not only because she was the eldest daughter, but also because she was the first of her siblings to marry.

The couple broke tradition by paying for their own wedding, instead of following the old world customs of the bride's family providing a dowry. Anna was forced to give up her job with Westinghouse, because she belonged to a union whose bylaws stated that married women were not allowed to continue working there. Her boss even tried to get her to keep the wedding a secret, but she could not do so since her husband-to-be wanted the traditional Slovak ceremony and reception and wanted a notice placed in the newspaper.

Even with the second generation, weddings were highly anticipated events and still involved as many family members as possible. The only one of Anna's siblings not in attendance was John Jr. who was still serving in the U.S. Navy at the time. Her other siblings were still quite young; Joe and Mike were teenagers; Helen was 12-years-old; Gerry was eight, and Margie only four. Helen recalled how pretty her sister looked in her white satin wedding gown with the long train and veil that cascaded down to her waist and how handsome her new brother-in-law was in his black tuxedo, which complemented his blond wavy hair. The wedding party was small and consisted of family and friends. John's sister, Betty served as Anna's matron of honor and his cousin, Ed Bavolar, was the best man. The attendants included Anna's cousin, Alice Yuhasz and friend, Mary Mikita; John's cousin, George Alzo, and his best friend John "Whitey" Petrisko.

It must have been an emotional time for Verona as she watched her daughter marry; perhaps she reflected back on her own wedding day and the absence of her own mother. Now, she was fortunate to be with her daughter, to offer advice and support and to ensure that the Slovak traditions were carried on as far as the New World would permit.

By marrying in the Greek Catholic Church, Anna went through some of the same rituals and traditions as her mother did on her wedding day. Anna and Johnny's marriage involved a mixture of Slovak and American wedding customs. Those Slovak traditions included the couple wearing wreathes on their heads during the marriage ceremony, but the ceremony differed a bit from the usual pattern in that they were unable to get married during the actual mass due to the church celebrating a holy day, so the couple attended mass in the morning and were married in the afternoon. There were other customs that were kept, such as the couple asking for a blessing before they entered their parents' homes, while the family threw pennies on the porch to ensure good luck to the couple. These customs were insisted on more by Johnny's relatives than Anna's, but did not carry the same significance as when their own parents married. The customs of the old world were associated with material scarcity, marriage as necessity and were reflections of rural life, a slow-paced, non-industrial society with marriage as a basis for acquiring property and perpetuating economic survival, especially for future descendants. The material abundance of America, however, indicated it was an industrial society in which marriage was no longer a necessity and marriage customs often reflected this lifestyle. With second generation Slovaks, like my parents, love became a more important factor.

The reception was held at the Hungarian Club in Duquesne. Anna's family spent several days cooking the *kolbassi* and sauerkraut, *holupki* (stuffed cabbage), *pirohi*, pickled beets, potatoes, and the other same traditional foods that were served at her mother's wedding. After dinner, an orchestra played live music and everyone danced. Anna danced the traditional bridal dance as her mother had done some 20 years earlier. At the end of the bridal dance, Anna's mother removed her daughter's veil, to signify that Anna was now a married woman, but the full ritual of the capping ceremony her mother went through was omitted. The significance of this and other rituals was lost in modern society and such adaptation offered the fun of tradition without any consequences suffered in real life.

There was also plenty of whiskey and beer, and Anna's father had too much to drink. He asked the band leader to play a polka so that he could dance with his daughter, and when he refused, Jánoš got angry and kept shouting that it was his daughter's wedding and "the lousy son-of-a-bitch wouldn't even play a song for him." Knowing their father's temper, Anna feared that a bloody fight might break out. Instead, after a few more drinks, Jánoš simply left his daughter's reception and walked home.

The newly married couple did not take a honeymoon. Johnny had planned a trip for them to Washington D.C., but Anna would not go because she was afraid that her father, angry over the incident with the band, would fall into one of his drunken rages and hurt her mother while she was away.

When second generation Slovaks married, they usually lived with their spouses in the paternal home to save up for a place of their own. As newlyweds my mother and father instead moved in with her parents in the house on Hill Street. The couple had their own bedroom and use of the kitchen, but her parents' home was still crowded since all the children except for John Jr. still lived there. After a few months, the couple went to live next door with Johnny' parents, because their home was less crowded. Johnny's sister, Betty still lived there and was pregnant with her second child. A few months later Anna discovered that she too was pregnant, so she and Johnny moved back to the Figlar household for a short time until they were eventually able to afford to rent a place of their own, then they moved a few blocks away to High Street.

Anna and Johnny eagerly anticipated the birth of their first child who was to be born the following October. During her pregnancy, Anna's blood pressure rose to levels which caused her doctor to be concerned and warned Anna of the possible dangers of carrying the baby full term. He suggested that she have an abortion to avoid having a child with physical or mental deformities, or risk losing her own life while giving birth. Anna went to see another doctor who offered the same prognosis, but Anna refused to have an abortion because her faith did not permit it and she believed it was morally wrong. Anna's mother offered comfort to her daughter and told her to pray and to "leave things in God's hands."

Approximately six months into her pregnancy, Anna began hemorrhaging and had to be taken into the hospital. The baby girl was stillborn. It was June, and Johnny's sister, Betty had just given birth to a healthy baby girl. Anna was devastated at losing her own daughter. She became depressed and even begged her husband to leave her, but he would not. He suggested she see another doctor for advice on whether they could try for another child. The doctor was not optimistic given Anna's hypertension and suggested the couple adopt. Johnny did not like the idea of adoption and said that if they could not have children of their own that he did not want anyone else's baby.

In 1949, Anna's doctor sent her to the Cleveland Clinic in August for a sympathectomy operation—a fairly new procedure designed to help regulate high blood pressure. While she did not like the idea of having an operation, Anna decided it was the best course, especially if she hoped to conceive again. Anna recalls how if it had not been for her mother, she might not have made it through that difficult time in her life. Verona encouraged her daughter to maintain her faith in God and find the strength to stay in her marriage even if she was unable to have children. The two women were closer to one another at that point in Anna's life than they were all those years while she was growing up.

The relationship with her daughter helped provide stability for Verona as she watched her two younger sons, Joe and Mike, venture out on their own. Joe had hoped to go to college, but because of their working class economic status his parents could not afford to finance any further education for their children after the twelfth grade. Joe's dilemma was delayed somewhat as he was drafted after graduation, and spent a few years in the paratroopers. When he came out of the service, Joe, like many Slovak men of the second generation, found his ticket to higher education through sports, earning a football scholarship to Case Western Reserve University. While in high school, Joe was a star fullback on the Duquesne High football team. For Joe, sports provided for easier assimilation than work or other areas of life. Prejudice toward early Slavic immigrants did not entirely disappear with successive generations, those of the second generation often found it difficult to fit into the workplace stereotype of "hunky" was perpetuated by American bosses despite the fact that young people no longer spoke with foreign accents and understood and practiced American ways.

Mike, who was three years younger than Joe, wanted to follow his brother to Cleveland and go to school there, as opposed to following his father to the steel mill. But before he had a chance to start school, he was drafted into the army and served in the Korean War.

With the boys gone, Anna helped her mother look after the three youngest girls, Helen, Gerry and Margie. Although Anna no longer lived at home, her concern for her mother did not stop, and she frequently visited the house on Hill Street. Helen viewed her sister Anna as a "second party disciplinarian" for her parents. Verona was always afraid that she was going to get in trouble with

Jánoš, so she asked Anna to watch out for them, and she became her mother's assistant as far as discipline was concerned. Helen was the oldest of the three younger girls and felt that she was watched most, especially when she became old enough to date. In high school she began to date Nick Lizanov who often visited her at home. Anna, knowing their father would be angered if he came home from work to find Nick there, would constantly have to chase Nick home. The less they provoked Jánoš, the better off they would all be. Gerry was younger and was always impressed the generosity of her older sister. Anna worked in McKeesport and when she would stop after work to see her parents, she would bring the girls a treat, usually cookies such as huge lady locks (large, flaky pastries filled with whipped cream). It was the youngest, Margie, over whom Anna had the most influence. In fact, Margie grew up thinking of Anna as a second mother, rather than a sister. Verona was ashamed at having a baby so late in life, and whenever Margie wanted Verona to go to an event at school, Verona would say, "You take Anka. I can't go, I'm too old—older than the other mothers." Margie would cry and say to her mother, "Anka can come, but I want you to come too, you're my mother." Whenever the three of them would go out shopping, Verona let strangers believe that Margie was her granddaughter, not her daughter.

Verona was not quite 50, but she still believed she was too old to have a child Margie's age. The years of hard work were reflected in her physical appearance—in her sunken eyes and the wrinkles on her face. Even then she still had to endure her husband's drinking and abusive behavior; her only consolation was that the violent episodes were becoming less frequent as her husband grew older. But when the incidents did occur, they followed the usual pattern.

One particular evening he was impossible to control. It was around 1956 and the mill was on strike. John, Jr. was home on leave from the Navy. Joe and Mike were home as well. Both of them now lived in Cleveland. Mike had gone there after he was discharged from the service and went back to Cleveland, found a job and intended to once again go to school. The boys found that despite the fact they all moved on, their father had not changed; he was still prone to drinking spells and abusive behavior toward their mother or anyone who got in his way.

Jánoš must have spent several hours "up the corner" and when he came home was extremely argumentative and began pounding on the table, throwing chairs, and swinging wildly at anyone who stepped in front of him. Somebody called the police. This was the second time such action was taken. The two police officers who responded were friends of the family, and they took Jánoš down to the jail so he could cool off; they wanted to scare him.

This was the last violent outburst that touched the family. The children, now adults or young adults, became less tolerant of their father's drinking and violent outbursts, and their resentment toward him began to surface. The children even suggested to their mother that she leave him, but she would not listen. Back then they did not have marriage counselors as they do today. If Verona had chosen to speak of her problems with her husband, she most likely would have gone to her priest for advice because of her religious conviction. It is likely that the priest would have told her to try to put up with the situation and suggest she and her husband get to know one another better and possibly that she should sometimes give in when he feels he is right.

Verona's relationship with her husband was a matter she essentially kept private and did not discuss even with her children. While it seems that the violent situations such as those my grandfather initiated could cause the breakup of many marriages today, back then it was not as easy or common for couples to divorce. Poverty and crowded living conditions placed additional strains on marriages, as did the presence of boarders in the household. Many unemployed husbands who might have held to their responsibilities due to social pressure in their homeland deserted their families in America. Many women were left without food for their children or with unpaid rent or outstanding debts to the grocer or butcher.

While her husband was demanding and her living conditions tumultuous at times, my grandmother may have been considered fortunate in that she was not left alone or widowed as

92

many 19th and 20th century immigrant women had been due to desertion or the death of their husbands or because of disease or industrial accidents. There were numerous occasions when her sons and daughters tried to talk her into consulting a lawyer. They kept telling her she did not have to live in the violent situation in which she often found herself. She was now in a country where she did not have to put up with abuse and fighting all of the time. But Verona would not hear of it. She was a believer in the old ways of, "I'm married to him, I stay with him, 'til death do us part." For her personally, divorce was not an option. In Orthodox faith, divorce was allowed only in case of adultery with the right to remarry granted to the innocent party. Occasionally divorce was allowed for other reasons (malicious desertion) with a marriage permitted even for the guilty party after a period of penance. Verona believed that the vows she took in front of God and her family and friends on her wedding day were sacred and the words "the husband is the head of the wife," must have echoed in her head at times when her children mentioned anything about her leaving their father.

Around this time, one by one the younger children began to move away and build their own lives. John was discharged from the Navy, earned a degree from the Art Institute of Pittsburgh and became a commercial artist for the Reuben-Donnelly company in Pittsburgh. He also met and married Virginia Morone and they settled in the Hazelwood section of Pittsburgh. Joe remained in Cleveland and married Antoinette Ciccia, eventually settling in the suburb of Lakewood. Mike also remained in Cleveland where he went to college for a few semesters, but then dropped out and took a job on the railroad. He met Laurel Vogelmuth and they married and settled in Brookpark. Helen and Gerry went to work and eventually married. Helen wed Nick Lizanov and eventually settled about 15 minutes from Duquesne in West Mifflin. Gerry married Mickey Abbott and after living in Erie, Pennsylvania for a time, moved back to Pittsburgh. Margie was the only sibling who stayed at home. Then, in 1971, she married Ben Augenstein.

Anna and Johnny stayed in Duquesne. In 1962, one year after Johnny's father had died from an unexpected heart attack, the couple purchased a home on Wool Street from Johnny's cousin. It was a five-room row house which consisted of a kitchen, living room, two small bedrooms, a bathroom and a basement, connected on the outside to two other homes; one on each side. Many years earlier it had been a company owned house. As far as my mother was concerned, the location was perfect because it was only three blocks up the hill from her parents' house on Hill Street. She wanted to be nearby since her parents were getting older so that she could help take care of them.

As Jánoš neared retirement age, his health began to fail. His legs ached almost all the time due to poor circulation. He no longer made frequent stops at the Union Grill. He would visit the bar only occasionally on afternoons when he knew his buddies would be there for a card game. But his drinking slowed down; his body could not take the amounts of alcohol that it used to when he was a younger man. Although he was less violent physically, he still made demands on my grandmother to attend to his needs— especially where serving him meals and cleaning up after him were concerned. His status as an American citizen and even his adaptation to some aspects of American culture did not take away his belief system or old world values. She continued to serve him, but also began turning her attention elsewhere. She began to focus on her grandchildren.

CHAPTER TWELVE
A GRANDDAUGHTER'S REFLECTION

    I grew up in a world that was half American and half Slovak. My daily life reflected an upbringing that was predominantly American: I spoke English and ate American foods such as hamburgers and French fries, watched television, rode a bus to school, traveled by car everywhere else, and talked on the telephone. I learned the pledge of allegiance and national anthem in school. Yet I was very much a part of a Slovak heritage embedded in tradition passed on to me mostly by my grandmother and somewhat by my mother. As a child I was unaware of the significance of the culture and its practices, but it was always present in the foods my grandmother prepared, the language she spoke and the holiday customs she observed.

    I was born on December 5, 1964, and named Lisa Ann; Lisa, which means "consecrated to God," after my father's mother, Elisabeth, and Ann for my mother. At the time of my birth, my grandmother was 65 years old. There is a photograph of my grandparents with me, taken on the day of my baptism. Grandma and Grandpap are standing inside the living room in front of the door of my parents' house and Grandma is holding me in a white blanket securely in her arms. She is full-figured and wearing a modest navy and white print, short-sleeve dress with a V-neckline and no collar. Her lips are closed together and crinkled up to form a tiny smile. Grandpap is wearing a white shirt with gray pants and a gray tie. His hair is cropped close to his head and he is smiling with a look of pride. I was not the first grandchild—but I was the child of their first-born, the daughter who at 39, finally gave birth after believing for 16 years she could not have children. I believe that when Grandma held me that first time, a bond formed, one that tied us together, not just by blood lines, but also by a rich heritage that would shape my life in ways I would not fully realize until many years later, such as through the passing on of certain personality traits, inner qualities, values, and aversions attributed as particular to the Slovak people. While it wouldn't have occurred to her at the time, I was also the third generation of Slovak women, the one who would experience growing up in a world more American than Slovak (even my first and middle names were given to sound more American than Slovak), filled with experiences and opportunities my grandmother could never imagine, the one who would have the responsibility of carrying the rich cultural traditions and legacy of the close family bonds into the next century.

Over time, every nationality or ethnic group has been identified as having a certain traits, such as common physiological characteristics, a common religion, language, historical and cultural heritage, which constitute a national character or identity. Slovaks have been characterized as deeply religious, with a spiritual strength and the capacity to hope, resist and grow, an inner vitality reflected in daily life by patience and perseverance, and artistically endowed (expressing themselves through art, poetry and song and dance). They have also been described as modest, hospitable, diligent in their work (with both male and female taking pride in their daily chores or tasks, no matter how simple or mundane), and an unfailing devotion to God, work and family. Looking back I remember my grandparents exhibited all of these traits in one form or another and I believe that these traits were passed on to me through the way I was raised.

As a young child, I recall spending more time at my grandparents' house than my own. By this time, my grandparents were over 70 years old and began to suffer health problems. Grandpap's poor circulation in his legs made it difficult for him to move around, and Grandma suffered from asthma, and ultimately a heart condition. Since they could not get around on their own, my mother spent a great deal of her free time taking care of their personal business for them: doing their banking and grocery shopping, cleaning their house and paying their bills. This was after her sister Margie had married and moved to a home of her own. Margie, as well as Helen and Gerry helped out when they could, but lived farther away.

As a family we spent many evenings and most weekends with my grandparents. Sometimes I would spend time with them

96

alone, when my mother worked one evening during the week and usually on Saturday as a secretary for an optometrist, and my father worked overtime on the railroad or took outside carpentry jobs.

During these times, I had little interaction with my grandfather. I remember him only as a short, stocky, old man, who was bald except for the thinning gray hair at the sides and walked with a cane. He used to sit at the kitchen table and roll his own cigarettes, carefully filling each paper with tobacco from the turquoise Bugler can, and play solitaire or "Beat the Devil," as he liked to call it, for hours at a time. He would call out to Grandma in Slovak and she would respond with a plate of food or a shot glass of Kassers 51 whiskey (he always bought Kasser's because it was available by the quart, while many of the other brands were sold by the pint) that she would place next to his ashtray.

I mostly remember my grandmother in the kitchen, where she would make what seemed bottomless pots of chicken and vegetable soup and bake homemade buns, golden brown and dusted with flour. The buns smelled so good; they made my mouth water. Grandma was aware of how much I liked them and she would hide two or three for me under a clean dish towel. She also would make my favorite dish, *palacinka*, the Slovak version of a crepe, that we rolled up with cottage cheese and jelly, then drizzled with melted butter.

When not in the kitchen Grandma would sit in the living room, sip hot tea with milk and sugar and watch various programs on the color television. Although she had difficulty understanding the shows, she seemed to delight in them anyway. She enjoyed her "stories" (the soap operas), "Search for Tomorrow" and "The Guiding Light." On weekday evenings, she often watched the British comedy "Benny Hill" or re-runs of "Gunsmoke," and on Saturday evening, "Lawrence Welk." On Sunday afternoon she would usually wash her hair in the bathroom sink. Sometimes I would catch a glimpse of her as she brushed it. I thought her dark hair, marbled with gray, was beautiful. It took her what seemed a long time to brush her hair, which fell naturally down to her waist, although she usually wore it pulled back and braided, pinned up behind her head.

Grandma spoke broken English, but most often she spoke Slovak, a language I did not understand and failed to learn.

While my mother knew both Slovak and English, that was not the case with me. I made only one attempt at learning Slovak. One summer, my father's sister, a nun who lived in Texas, came home for a visit and tried to teach me. We started with numbers. Auntie would say them and I would repeat: *jeden, dva, tri,/styri, pät', sest',/ sédem, osem, devät', desát*. I seem to recall that we covered the numbers one to twenty in that first lesson, but to this day, all I can remember is one to ten. Then we tried to move on to other words and even prayers like the "Lord's Prayer."

Unlike English, every letter in the Slavic alphabet corresponds to a distinct sound, which is generally the same, with a few exceptions. The language contains specific components such as diacritical marks (special accent marks to show which of many pronunciations to use for each vowel), case endings for nouns and conjugation endings for verbs. While there is one standard written form of Slovak, a variety of regional dialects exist in Slovakia, my grandmother's being just one of them. To me, the words sounded nasal, like being stuffed up with a cold, and the vowels were difficult to pronounce.

This brief lesson was the extent of my learning Slovak. My aunt went back to Texas, and nobody followed up on what she had taught me. As a child, the interest on my part was momentary. It was something new and different at the time, but when not encouraged to keep learning, I forgot all about this other language.

The earliest Slovak immigrants identified themselves in terms of language and religion. My grandmother, like others of the first generation, continued to speak Slovak at home, with her friends, at church or family celebrations. Her children (particularly the older ones), although raised to speak the language, preferred to speak English among themselves. As a child, I remember hearing my grandmother and mother talk for hours on end in Slovak and wondered what it was they were saying to one another. I imagined them as friends. Did my grandmother confide in my mother? Did my mother confide in my grandmother? Were they sharing some secret that I was not entitled to know?

The use of Slovak generally declined in the 1940s and 1950s as many of the first generation died off. The second generation saw no advantage in teaching Slovak to their children and felt more comfortable speaking English. It has been reported that among the grandchildren and great-grandchildren of the Slovak immigrants, that few to almost none can speak the Slovak language and that with few exceptions, have lost the language completely.

While the Slovak language was something not passed on to me, religion, the other area with which Slovaks identified, was a part of my life since the time I started first grade through high school. During that time my religion and my education were intertwined.

I did not go to the public school. Instead, my mother enrolled me in the school that was affiliated with our church, Duquesne Catholic. Years ago, when my father went there, the school was known as Holy Trinity, or as he referred to it, "Hunky Tech" because of the predominant number of Slovak children enrolled there. Over the years, however, enrollment declined sufficiently enough that Holy Trinity merged with the other two Roman Catholic churches in Duquesne to form the Duquesne Catholic School. When she was growing up my mother did not have the chance to experience a religious education. At that time, religion and community size tended to play a role in the selection of a school among the first two generations of Slovaks. When it came time to select a school for me, the opportunity for a Catholic education was readily available and mother insisted on it. In earlier days, parochial schools for the Roman Catholic Slovaks were a way to ensure that the children preserved their language and ethnicity and fulfilled the goal of having children raised in a moral Slovak atmosphere. In my case, I did not learn the Slovak language or much about the culture in school, but the required attendance at weekly mass and catechism classes perpetuated the moral and religious principles my mother had hoped I would receive.

In fact, my mother saw to it that I had a strict religious upbringing, making sure I attended church each week and said my prayers every night, just as her mother had done with her when she was young. The only difference was that I was being raised Roman Catholic instead of Greek Catholic. One would think that my Grandmother would have objected to our affiliation with the Roman Catholic church, but she never vocalized any objections. I believe that this was because Grandma's faith went beyond an allegiance to a particular denomination or church affiliation. She was "religious" in the purest sense and what mattered most to her was that her children and grandchildren grew up believing in God; how they worshipped was their business. It didn't matter whether they went to the Greek or Roman Catholic or Protestant church, just as long as they went. Grandma's idea was quite basic: if you did not go to church, then you did not go anywhere else on Sunday. My mother perpetuated this same belief while I was growing up. Grandma's devotion to God remained even though her health would not permit her to attend mass. On Sunday mornings Grandma listened to a Greek Catholic church service conducted in Slovak on the radio. She would sit quietly by the kitchen window, her head bowed and her hands folded in her lap. I marveled at her dedication to her faith, something that she passed on to my mother.

After devotion to God, devotion to family was next in importance to my grandmother. This devotion was instilled in my mother. She showed her dedication to my grandparents, especially my grandmother, through her desire to take care of them.

When I was seven years old, my grandmother had suffered a blood clot to her leg, which made it difficult for her to move around. She rarely climbed the steep flight of stairs to the three bedrooms or bathroom on the second floor of her home. She confined her movements to the front living room, the kitchen and the bedroom in between which had previously served as a dining area. A small bathroom with only a toilet and sink was also installed off of the kitchen. Mother constantly worried about Grandma and spent more of her free time attending to her needs, and made the decision to continue living near my grandparents.

Although I never fully understood the relationship that my mother shared with my grandmother, as I grew older I somehow sensed a close bond between the two women that fascinated me.

My parents talked about moving only once. In 1965, my mother's sister Helen and her husband, Nick, had bought a lot in a new plan of homes about 15 minutes away in West Mifflin so that their daughter, Lynne, could attend school in the more reputable West Mifflin district. Aunt Helen suggested that my mother and father buy the lot next door, but my father was not so keen to move because it would increase his seven minute commute to the Union Railroad where he worked but would have made the sacrifice, had my mother insisted they move. Although all of my mother's siblings had settled outside of Duquesne, she wanted to stay there because she was reluctant to leave her parents.

No matter what choices her siblings made, my mother's strong ties to her parents remained, and she was convinced that as long as they were alive, she had to be near them; she was afraid that they might need her and she would not be there for them. She even felt guilty because she could not be there for my grandmother more often than she was, a guilt which I could not comprehend at the time since she stopped at my grandmother's house practically every day and the times she could not stop, she called.

I can't help but think that my grandmother felt a sense of guilt when she decided to leave her own mother behind in Slovakia some 40 years earlier. She once told my mother about her sadness concerning her departure. Grandma never saw her mother again once she left for America, and when her mother died many years after that, she did not go back to attend her funeral. Instead, she grieved at a distance with only her memories to comfort her. My own mother's circumstances were different; the economic and political reasons which separated my grandmother from her family did not exist for my mother. If she had made the decision to move, she would have been just 15 minutes away, not across the ocean, and could visit with her mother any time she wished. But the sense of family obligation penetrated my mother's conscience. From childhood she had learned to protect her mother, mostly from her father's rage and violent outbursts. As an adult, this protective

101

instinct stayed with her: she desired to guard her mother from any and all painful experiences that might occur.

Perhaps my mother's desire to stay near her parents went back to the beliefs of the early Slavic immigrants that the family formed the heart of their community. Slovak immigrants and their families often lived in extended families with parents, grandparents, children, aunts, uncles, cousins and in-laws all under the same roof. First immigrants often extended their families even further by taking in boarders, as my own grandparents had done. For them, the family was a survival mechanism, an important structure in the early years of adjustment to a new culture.

The Slavic family has been distinguished historically by stability and mutual reciprocity between the generations. In the Slavic conception of family, nourishing takes place with the elderly and the children and there is reciprocal support among the generations.

After my grandmother suffered the blood clot, my mother and her siblings began to rally around her to help with preparing meals for my grandfather and cleaning her large house. My Aunt Gerry would come with her husband and two boys, my Uncle John with his wife and three children, and my Aunt Margie who did not have any children at that time. The men would walk up to the Union Grill bar (they referred to it as going "up the corner") to have a few shots of whiskey and some beers, and brought back fish sandwiches for dinner, as Fridays were always meatless for Catholics. We also had some type of "Slovak" dish, usually *haluski*, a hot dish of noodles tossed with cooked cabbage.

After supper, the women sat at the kitchen table and talked over coffee and dessert, usually an apple or lemon pie Grandma had made, while the men played cards in the next room and broke out the whiskey Grandpap had stashed under the kitchen sink. My cousins and I played games in the basement. Our Friday nights were about family togetherness and the celebration of our heritage with food and tradition.

Despite earning American citizenship, my grandparents perpetuated the idea that family was the most important aspect in one's life, no matter how many disputes you had, what sorrows or troubles transpired. In coming together to care for my grandparents, a feeling of intimacy and responsibility was developed between the generations, and because of their influence, a sense of family interdependency was instilled in all of us.

In 1973, my grandfather became bedridden. Grandma could not take care of him so my mother spent many days and nights at my grandparents' house. Grandma's house became my second home. Mother would walk me a few blocks up Crawford street so that I could catch my school bus in the morning and would meet me there when I was dropped off in the afternoon. Since I was only nine years old at the time, I don't remember much about Grandpap's illness except that he used to yell out and curse (mostly in Slovak) because he was in pain. He eventually went to a nursing home and died from a blood clot to his heart in 1974.

Grandma confided in my mother that before my grandfather died he told her he was sorry for all that he did to her. She explained to my mother how my grandfather cried and begged her forgiveness. He also wanted his children to forgive him, and even confessed to a priest so that he could have God's forgiveness as well, despite the fact that for most of his adult life he had no use for priests. Verona had since joined the Russian Orthodox church in Duquesne because the Greek Catholics had started following the American dates for holy days such as Christmas and Easter and she did not want to follow this change.

Mother told me that she, herself, was able to forgive her father. In fact, she was deeply saddened by his death. In the Russian Orthodox church, the casket is reopened during the funeral mass and the living say their final good-byes in a procession in front of the casket. The image of my mother throwing her arms around my grandfather as he lay in the casket, and weeping loudly, will never leave my memory.

Throughout the next ten years Grandma lived alone. No matter how my mother or her siblings pleaded with her to sell her house and live with one of them she would not do so. The logical move would have been with Helen or Gerry because their homes were single level and Grandma would not have to climb the stairs which she would have had to do living in our house. The family

103

worried about Grandma not just because of her failing health, but also because the house was in a location prone to crime, especially robberies. But Grandma refused to leave. She always said, "I am not by myself, the Lord is here with me and will take care of me."

Grandma still lived in her own house when I graduated from high school in June 1983. There is a photograph of my grandmother, my mother and me on graduation day. I am standing between the two women in my cap and gown. Grandma looks small and frail in a flowered dress and dark blue sweater. She is wearing glasses and her hair, now almost completely gray, is pulled back away from her face and braided in a knot behind her head. Mother has on a purple and white dress and has her arm around me. I know that Mother had a real sense of pride that I graduated with top honors from high school and would be going to college—an opportunity which neither she nor her mother had as young women. Although Grandma never said it, I could tell from the look on her face that she too was proud because I would be going to college. The day I left for West Virginia Wesleyan College, she hugged me and put a twenty-dollar bill in my pocket. She was always giving me money and even when I refused she insisted I take it. I remember her face in the window as she waved good-bye to me. After that I saw her only on holidays and during summer vacations. Grandma's health declined drastically and after being in and out of the hospital for various reasons, she was no longer able to live alone. She stayed with both my Aunt Gerry and Aunt Helen for extended periods. During Christmas of my sophomore year, Grandma took ill and was put in the hospital because she was having difficulty breathing and her heart was weak. She died on the 29th of December. Mother said she seemed to wait for me to come home to see her one more time and also for the family to celebrate Christmas Eve together, before passing away. We buried her on New Year's Day.

In looking back I realize that Grandma was the glue that held our family together. When she died, there was an underlying fear that with her gone perhaps the family would break apart. She was the center for so many years, and we were afraid that the void she left might be the thing to separate us. Ironically, her spirit, love, and her belief of "family is everything" that she instilled in her children actually served to keep us together.

In thinking about Grandma's death, I believe that somehow it sealed the death of the first generation, and in a way the death of the family's Slovak heritage. It seems coincidental that her death came around the time of the decline of the steel era in Pittsburgh and the working class culture that she and her husband became a part of fifty years earlier. The Duquesne Works officially closed in 1984, the same year Grandma died. Perhaps this was an omen for things to come—of a generation and a working class culture that was dying out as well.

As a child I remember summer evenings, standing on the back porch of Grandma and Pap-pap Figlar's two-story house on Hill Street. The porch faced the steel mill and I would watch the blue and orange flames, which burned from the largest blast furnace, which the Duquesne residents affectionately named "Dorothy." The flames seemed to dance as they emitted their bright light in the darkened sky. At the time I did not realize the significance of the mill to my family. The flames were something interesting for me to watch, but I did not understand that behind the pretty colors there existed an industrial giant, a fiery hell which consumed the lives of men like my grandfather, forcing them to work too hard and too much, and often times pushing them to drink more than they should have or to release their bottled frustrations by beating their wives and children.

The flames from Dorothy are gone. So are my grandparents. Their house was sold to a woman whom I never met. The outside of the house no longer looks as it did when my grandparents owned it. The front porch where Grandma used to sit on her glider and wait for her children and grandchildren to visit, or a neighbor to pass by, is now enclosed with white aluminum siding. There are no children running back and forth between the side door and backyard, as my cousins and I used to do when we played hide-and-seek.

The houses in the surrounding blocks are now rundown or neglected; nothing but broken windows, faded paint, and crumbled steps. The neighborhood stores where my grandmother used to

105

walk to do her shopping are now boarded up, "CLOSED," and the ethnic churches she attended are threatened by consolidation and closure. There are drive-by shootings, drug raids and robberies, and people dare not walk alone, day or night, and many must even be afraid to sit on their own front porches.

In Duquesne as in many of the other industrial cites throughout the northeast, the old Slovak neighborhoods still house what is left of the first two generations of blue-collar workers, but the subsequent generations who became white-collar workers have disappeared to the suburbs nearby. This was especially true in Duquesne, as the young men opted not to labor in the mills as their fathers and grandfathers did and began to move toward alternative employment, and as educational opportunities opened up to young women like myself, calling those of us from the third generation away to other areas.

I wonder what my grandmother would think of Duquesne today? The mill her husband labored in for over thirty years now stands silent and lifeless in decay, hunks of rusted metal covered by dust, debris and weeds. Unemployment plagues most of the remaining residents. Even the ore bridge where my grandfather spent many hours of his working day was destroyed in order to make way for a new business park. All it took was some dynamite and a few minutes to wipe out that history, and in a way, a part of me is gone forever in that blast.

The Duquesne that welcomed my grandmother over 80 years ago is nothing but a memory captured in the minds of those who knew it back then, or in faded newspaper clippings stashed away in the file cabinets of the local libraries. The past is vanishing in ways both visible and invisible: by each piece of the old blast furnaces or millsite buildings that are blown up, cleared away and paved over with concrete or blacktop; by each descendant of those first immigrants who move away People like me.

For my grandmother, who after coming through Ellis Island looked forward to going to Duquesne, the place held the promise of a new life. Economic conditions and geographical reality caused my grandmother to leave the place where she grew up, and it was in Duquesne where my grandmother made a new home, where she lived and worked among those of both Slavic descent and those of various other backgrounds, where she learned how to be an American. Unlike my grandmother, who could not wait to get to Duquesne, I could not wait to get out.

In December 1995, I left Duquesne to pursue a job opportunity in Ithaca, New York. Although the prospect of going away appealed to me, I went through the same struggles my own mother had, as the knowledge that my parents were older and my father in ill health, tugged at me to stay. I felt like Mother did about Grandma: I did not want to leave. I wanted to stay and take care of them. But the bond that kept my mother in Duquesne was not powerful enough to keep me. Perhaps it was because circumstances were different, the world did not seem so big now and New York not so far away. At the time I rationalized my departure with the idea that I could return to Duquesne via a few hours drive in my car, or a brief plane ride. My mother understood my need to go, just as my great-grandmother understood my grandmother's need so many years before. Although there are significant differences, I believe there are parallels between the experiences of my grandmother and my own experiences. In a way it was economic conditions and geographic realities influencing me to leave my hometown, and like Grandma, I went to live and work among people whose backgrounds are different from my own.

After I moved, my mother was once again stuck in the middle: afraid to stay, but too settled to leave. My mother and father had developed a sense of security in Duquesne. They owned their home and experienced close ties with friends, neighbors and their church, circumstances which were not all that different from those of the early immigrants. At that time, breaking those ties they grew up with and kept through adulthood, would have been an incredibly difficult thing to do.

The women of my family genuinely cared for one another, and it was because of the nurturing between my mother and grandmother that I grew up with a real sense of family belonging and bonding. When I think of the differences between our three

107

lives, I find I must recognize that I owe most of who I am to my mother and my grandmother. These two women passed on to me traits that I value such as devotion to family and a strong work ethic, which prompts me to take pride in the work that I do and desire to be recognized for a job well-done. In addition, I believe that I have inherited a kind of creativity. While my mother and grandmother demonstrated their creativity through cooking, with the ability to make elaborate dishes and bake wonderful mouth-watering pastries, I express myself creatively through writing.

Despite the differences in quality of life, it appears that between the generations one thing remained constant: What mothers wanted most for their daughters. My mother recalled that her own mother wanted her children to grow up healthy and that if they grew up to be fine young men and women, she could be proud of them. She wanted them to get good jobs, get married, have their own families and live a good life. The most important lesson she taught to each of her children was "be a good person." When I asked my mother what it was she wanted for me, she went a step further saying that she wanted material things for me. While Mother believed that she had more opportunities to make my life better, she reflected: "Most certainly my mother couldn't give me everything she would have liked to have given me and I am sure she felt the same with every one of us. And that's why I guess I try to give you everything that I was unable to have, because there is no way that they could possibly have done that for me. I had to go to work at a very early age if I wanted things, I didn't want that for you, I didn't want you to have to do that. I wanted things for you." Ultimately, however, my mother said she wanted me to be content, to be happy, and to be a good, loving and caring person.

As the third generation, I had the best of both worlds. I consider myself extremely fortunate to have grown up in America. I never lived through a depression or a war of the magnitude of the first two "world wars." I had few worries as my parents were financially in a position to provide a comfortable existence and even able to send me to private schools and to college. I was not forced to work as a teenager, and when I became an adult had my choice of occupations: In graduating from college, I achieved a success neither my grandmother nor my mother could claim. This education made it possible for me to attend graduate school and apply for professional jobs. I was free to choose to marry or not and to select a mate based on love. The old world customs were more of a novelty with no expectations to speak of. But I also grew up an only child without the large family presence my mother and grandmother both had.

My generation is farther removed from the Slavic heritage. Until a few years ago, I had a limited knowledge about the culture and how intertwined my grandmother's life was in that culture. As an immigrant she was part of a significant moment in history.

And yet, some sixteen years after Grandma's death, I find myself one more step removed from my heritage as my mother's generation has grown older, and faced with the knowledge that death is imminent. In 1995, my Uncle John died unexpectedly of a heart attack and with his death came the reality of the second generation passing away. His death came as a shock to my mother and her siblings. At least with Grandma and Grandpap, who were in ill health, they were prepared, but the death of one of their own generation was even more difficult to accept. I also believe that Uncle John's death also signified another step away from our heritage. Despite John's efforts to rebel against his parents and their ways as a young man, when he became older, he fervently kept the Slovak traditions alive in his own home by preparing the ethnic foods my grandmother used to make and also by preserving the idea of "family" by starting an annual family reunion in 1967 with my Aunt Gerry and her husband.

This reunion is the last concrete way in which the generations of my family bond together and serves to draw us all back to Pittsburgh each year in July despite the distance separating us. While two of my mother's sisters, Gerry and Margie, and her sister-in-law, Ginny, still live in Pittsburgh, the remaining members of my family live out-of-state. My Aunt Helen and her husband moved to Texas, my two uncles, Joe and Mike (and their families), live in Cleveland. Most of the third generation, (my cousins and myself), now live in areas outside of Pittsburgh, some as far away as Florida, and Texas, and some as nearby as New

Jersey, New York, Ohio, or Northeastern Pennsylvania. I know that my grandmother would have been delighted to know that we make the effort to keep the family bonds intact.

The closeness I cherish in my own family can fully be attributed to my grandmother. Our annual reunion is a testimony to the value she placed on family. In today's society, it seems the exception for families to make an effort to come together every year. This reciprocity of feeling between the generations was something started with my grandmother and continued through my mother and her siblings. It is now up to us—the third generation— to see to it that this feeling of reciprocity between the generations does not die and to preserve our Slavic heritage and values in an ever-changing society that often contradicts rather than encourages such practices.

I ponder what this means for future generations. The family has grown now to the fourth generation. How do future generations carry on a heritage we barely know ourselves? The degree of assimilation into American society, which we have experienced, has put a distance between the two cultures. I can't help but question how many more generations will be removed before the practices and traditions of our Slovak culture dies out altogether? My own way of preserving my history is through these written words, but is this all I can do?

My grandmother made the journey to get to America, now I have set out on my own journey: to make sure that my grandmother's spirit like that of other Slovak immigrant women is kept alive and to reach future generations with the hope that they will come to appreciate what they learned and inherited from their Slovak ancestors, as I have realized what my grandmother has given to me.

EPILOGUE

December, 2000

My mother passed away on September 12, 2000 at the age of 75. She was living with me in Ithaca, New York at the time and had been hospitalized at the end of August after a number of medical complications had set in. Her death was not entirely unexpected, but still very difficult to accept. My mother had been ill since 1997 when she had triple bypass heart surgery and was simultaneously diagnosed with renal failure (kidney disease). For three years she underwent a three-day per week regimen of hemodialysis to stay alive—a procedure that took a toll on her both physically and emotionally.

My parents had moved in with me the previous February and I became my mother's primary caregiver. By taking on this responsibility I assumed many additional roles, nurse, banker, driver, advocate, while maintaining a full-time job and trying to continue other activities. Shortly before her passing, I took on further responsibility by administering her treatments at home via peritoneal dialysis (or PD). It required connecting her at night and disconnecting her in the morning and monitoring her vital signs carefully. I stood by and watched as my mother lost her quality of life and became more and more dependent on me.

My mother slipped in and out of coma during her final stay in the hospital. As I visited her the day after Labor Day, we had a few special moments together that will forever be emblazoned in my memory. The nurses had her sitting up in a chair and she had just finished eating her lunch. The lunch consisted mostly of liquids and pureed foods since a few days earlier she had experienced a severe choking spell and the doctors were concerned about possible aspiration to her lungs. She wanted something more substantial so I fed her a few grapes from my own packed lunch, which she seemed to enjoy. After she ate the last grape, I took her hand in mine and said to her, "Mom, I just want you to know that you are a good mother, the best," and then I hugged her. She responded, "And you are a good daughter. God blessed me with a wonderful daughter."

111

At that moment, I think I somehow sensed that my mother would not be with me much longer. In the next week, her condition worsened to the point that she was not able to communicate clearly, and eventually not at all. Looking back now, it was in those few moments on that September day that we said our goodbyes.

On several occasions throughout her illness my mother indicated to me that she was afraid to die. Although, my mother had a deep faith in God and was a devout Catholic, she was afraid of dying. One of her doctors mentioned that it usually isn't death that people are afraid of, but dying itself. Knowing this, I prayed that she would somehow come to terms with her fears and find peace in the process. Always stubborn and independent, my mother struggled and fought until the burdens became more than she could bear. Finally, she said to me, "Okay, honey, Okay..." and I knew that this was her way of letting go—she was telling me that she accepted what was happening and what was ahead.

The evening my mother passed away, I went to the hospital as I had done each night before. Her breathing was very slow and her face looked peaceful. I held her and cried. Before I left, I put a portable cassette player containing a tape of hymns next to her and positioned the earphones to her ear. I kissed her forehead and told her how much I loved her, then left to go home. An hour later, I received the phone call that my mother had passed on. She finally found peace and relief from all of her suffering.

I realize how my mother must have felt when she lost her own mother sixteen years before—her heart so heavy with sadness. The passing of my grandmother left a big void in my mother's life—she lost her mother and her friend. I now feel the same way.

But while her physical presence is gone, our connection has not been broken. All that she taught me—her spirit and love—live on through me. Mother's departure from this world has brought me another step away from heritage. When grandma died, my mother preserved the culture and was the matriarch who held the family together. I now feel a responsibility to keep her legacy alive. The surviving members of the second generation have indicated a desire to keep the traditions going and pass them on to future generations, and I believe that I also play an important role in seeing that obligation fulfilled.

At our 2000 family reunion (the final one my mother would attend), my aunts, uncles and cousins presented me with an engraved plaque, naming me the "official" family historian, which reads,

> *"For efforts in researching our family history and promoting present day togetherness."*

This plaque is more than just a keepsake to me. It is a constant reminder of the responsibility I have inherited from my grandmother and mother for keeping the family in touch, and for exploring and preserving the family's history.

I have attempted to carry out my responsibilities partially through writing this book. These written words serve to bind the three of us—my grandmother, my mother, and me—and metaphorically bring us back together again.

I see no more fitting way to honor these two women who have gone before and all they stood for and believed in than to record and share the heritage they have passed on to me.

To view additional photographs of people and places mentioned in this book, and a selected bibliography, please visit the *Three Slovak Women* Web site at:

http://www.members.tripod.com/tswbook

ABOUT THE AUTHOR

Lisa Alzo was raised in Duquesne, Pennsylvania and currently resides in Ithaca, New York. She earned a Master of Fine Arts degree in Nonfiction Writing from the University of Pittsburgh in 1997, and spent six years researching her family's history for *Three Slovak Women*.

Lisa has taught genealogy and writing courses in the Finger Lakes Region of Central New York, and has been an invited speaker for national conferences, genealogical and historical societies. She is the recipient of the 2002 Mary Zirin Prize given by the Association for Women in Slavic Studies to recognize the achievements of independent scholars and to encourage their continued scholarship and service in the field of Slavic Women's Studies.